The Case for
Christianity
ANSWER BOOK

LEE STROBEL

ZONDERVAN®

Requests for information should be addressed to:

Zondervan, *Grand Rapids, Michigan 49530*

Special thanks to Mark Mittelberg for his invaluable contribution to creating this book.

Any Internet addresses (websites, blogs, etc.) and telephone numbers printed in this book are offered as a resource. They are not intended in any way to be or imply an endorsement by Zondervan, nor does Zondervan vouch for the content of these sites and numbers for the life of this book.

Unless otherwise noted, Scripture quotations marked NIV are taken from the Holy Bible, New International Version®, NIV®. Copyright © 1973, 1978, 1984, 2011 by Biblica, Inc.™ Used by permission of Zondervan. All rights reserved worldwide. www.zondervan.com. Scripture quotations marked ESV are taken from THE ENGLISH STANDARD VERSION. © 2001 by Crossway Bibles, a division of Good News Publishers. Scripture quotations marked HCSB are from HOLMAN CHRISTIAN STANDARD BIBLE. © 1999, 2000, 2002, 2003 by Broadman and Holman Publishers. All rights reserved.

ISBN 978-0-310-33955-7

Printed in China

14 15 16 17 18 TIMS 7 6 5 4 3

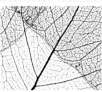

Contents

Prelude

Seeking Spiritual Answers

1

I have so many questions—and a few doubts—about the Christian faith. What should I do with them?

You are doing precisely what you need to do—you're being honest with yourself and open with your questions. That's the first step toward

finding answers. If you do the opposite—bottling up your concerns in the hopes they'll go away—then they'll just fester and infect your entire spiritual life.

Instead, let me urge you to follow the wisdom of Scripture. Jesus said, "Everyone who asks receives; the one who seeks finds; and to the one who knocks, the door will be opened" (Matt. 7:8). This echoes a principle in the Old Testament: "You will seek me and find me when you seek me with all your heart" (Jer. 29:13).

I've struggled with spiritual questions for most of my life, and in some ways I still do. It's an ongoing process to find answers that satisfy my heart and soul. But even bouts of doubt can show we're thinking and growing, rather than simply clinging to what we've been told.

As I described in *The Case for Christ*, my greatest season of spiritual introspection came after my wife, Leslie, announced that she had become a Christian. That was hard news for a skeptical journalist to hear! But it set in motion my own journey of asking tough questions—and

discovering unexpected answers. In the end, I concluded that it would take more faith for me to maintain my atheism than it would to become a Christian!

After almost two years of searching, I got on my knees and asked Jesus to forgive my sins and lead my life. It was a decision that changed everything; in fact, it was the pivotal moment of my life.

That decision, mixed with the research I did then and in the time since then, led me to a sense of confidence that there are satisfying answers to even our hardest questions. It's in that spirit that I write this book.

> Jesus stayed behind . . . sitting among
> the teachers, listening to them and
> asking them questions. Everyone
> who heard him was amazed at his
> understanding and his answers.
>
> LUKE 2:43, 46–47

2

Can you offer any practical
ideas on how to approach this
journey of finding answers?

Despite my initial reluctance to seeking spiritual truth, I did do one thing right. I set three principles for myself at the beginning of my search—guidelines that helped me then and that I trust will help you now, whether you're a skeptic or a Christian with questions.

1. Make the search a front-burner issue.

Finding answers is too important to approach casually or in sporadic snatches of time. I knew—and hope you agree—that these are urgent matters. Jeremiah 29:13 encourages us to seek God and his truth "with all your heart."

2. Keep an open mind and follow the evidence wherever it leads.

This principle had been drilled into me as a journalist, and it served me well in my spiritual journey. I had to strive for as much objectivity as I could muster, putting aside preconceived ideas and biases. Only then could meaningful answers be discerned. French philosopher Blaise Pascal said, "Truth is so obscure in these times, and falsehood so established, that unless we love the truth, we cannot know it."[1]

3. When the evidence is in, reach a verdict.

I knew these realities were far too important to ignore. If God is real, and if Jesus is who he claimed to be, then I would have to respond accordingly. Similarly, I hope you'll decide up front that when you weigh the facts, you'll allow the evidence to impact your own beliefs.

One more suggestion: *Ask the God you may not be sure about to guide you.* Just as Jesus honored the doubter who said, "I do believe; help me overcome my unbelief!" (Mark 9:24), he will honor your sincere request.

If you'll apply these principles and seek answers wholeheartedly, I'm confident you'll discover—as I did—that Jesus was indeed right when he promised:

"Ask and it will be given to you; seek and you will find; knock and the door will be opened to you. For everyone who asks receives; the one who seeks finds; and to the one who knocks, the door will be opened."

Jesus, in Matthew 7:7–8

3

How can I "keep an open mind" when I already have some strong opinions?

Great question! In spite of being trained as a journalist to follow the evidence wherever it leads, I know I came preloaded with a lot of misguided ideas and attitudes about the Christian faith.

I'd read just enough philosophy and history to find support for my skepticism—a fact here, a scientific theory there, a pithy quote, a clever catchphrase. Sure, I could see some gaps and inconsistencies in these skeptical arguments, but I had a strong motivation to ignore them: a self-serving, immoral lifestyle that I would be compelled to abandon if I were ever to change my views and become a follower of Jesus.

Then that fateful day came when Leslie announced she had become a Christian. Over time, however, the changes in my wife's attitudes prompted me to launch my own spiritual investigation.

That's when I finally determined to set aside my self-interest and prejudices as best I could. I exposed myself to sources of information that I knew would challenge me. I read books, interviewed experts, analyzed history, explored archaeology, studied ancient literature, and picked apart the Bible—constantly reminding myself to settle for nothing but the truth. This search eventually led me to Christ.

Maybe you too have been basing your spiritual outlook on the evidence you've observed around you or gleaned long ago from books, college professors, family members, or friends. But is your conclusion the best possible explanation of the evidence? If you were to dig deeper—to confront your presuppositions and systematically seek answers—what would you find?

To be selected for a jury you must affirm up front that you haven't formed any preconceptions

about the case. You are required to be open-minded and fair, drawing your conclusions from the facts and not your whims or prejudices. You are urged to thoughtfully consider the credibility of the witnesses, carefully sift the testimonies, and rigorously subject the evidence to common sense and logic.

That's a pretty good description of how we must approach our questions about God, the Bible, and the Christian faith—except this search for truth is far more important, because it can affect your soul and impact your eternity. This makes it all the more urgent to keep an open mind and to seek answers urgently.

"Therefore love truth . . ."

ZECHARIAH 8:19

Answers About God, the Creator

4

Are Christianity and science at odds?

Many people think that science and faith are archenemies, and that we must choose between the facts of scientific research and the superstitious folklore of religious tradition.

This was once my point of view. In high school I became convinced that the evidence for

Darwinian evolution had, in effect, put God out of a job. "Why do we need him anymore," I mused, "when we now know that life was formed through purely natural means?"

I would have agreed with physicist Steven Weinberg's statement: "One of the great achievements of science has been, if not to make it impossible for intelligent people to be religious, then at least to make it possible for them not to be religious."[1] For me, the initiation into science meant the graduation from belief in the supernatural. It was at that time that I began calling myself an atheist.

Today, my beliefs would be better summed up with this quote from nanoscientist James Tour of Rice University: "Only a rookie who knows nothing about science would say science takes away from faith. If you really study science, it will bring you closer to God."[2]

What I came to learn, as I described in *The Case for a Creator*, was that numerous strands of science—including cosmology, physics, astronomy, biochemistry, biology, and the study of

consciousness—all point in the same direction. With ever-increasing data, these disciplines indicate that there is an intelligent designer who has worked in miraculous ways to create and fine-tune the universe, and to populate it with a variety of living creatures—including humankind.

We'll explore a number of these areas in the answers that follow, but for now, suffice it to say that science and religion are not enemies. In fact, good science and true religion point to the same truths.

> The heavens declare the glory of God;
>> the skies proclaim the work of his
>> hands.
> Day after day they pour forth speech;
>> night after night they reveal
>> knowledge.
> They have no speech, they use no words;
>> no sound is heard from them.
> Yet their voice goes out into all the earth,
>> their words to the ends of the world.
>
> PSALM 19:1–4

5

Can We Prove God Exists?

It's interesting how one can grow up believing things as fundamental as God's existence, and yet feel wholly unprepared to defend those beliefs when put on the spot. That's a normal experience—not something to feel bad about. Let it motivate you to think more deeply about your faith, and thus it will be used for good.

What trips up many Christians is the over-reaching nature of the question itself. *Prove* is a strong word—one that sets the bar at an unrealistically high level. From my legal background I can tell you prosecutors almost never use that term alone. Instead, they attach it to four other important words. They'll say, "I'm going to prove *beyond a reasonable doubt*" that such-and-such happened.

In Scripture, we're told to "be prepared to give

an answer to everyone who asks you to give the reason for the hope that you have" (1 Peter 3:15). Giving an answer requires some forethought, but it's a lot easier than *proving* something!

So our first response to a friend asking this question might be, "No, I can't *prove* God exists, but I can offer some good reasons to believe in him." If your friend protests, ask him if he can "prove God *doesn't* exist." He'll quickly see that he doesn't have proof either.

What are some positive reasons we can give for believing in God (outside of quoting Bible verses, which most nonbelievers won't accept)? I asked that question of one of the world's leading defenders of Christianity, Dr. William Lane Craig, when I interviewed him for *The Case for Faith*. Here's a short version of his response.[3]

Reason #1: God Makes Sense of the Origin of the Universe

"Both philosophically and scientifically," Craig said, "I would argue that the universe and time itself had a beginning at some point in the

finite past . . . This is commonly known as the *Big Bang,* and it is accepted almost universally by scientists worldwide. But since something cannot just come out of nothing, there has to be a transcendent cause beyond space and time which brought the universe into being."

Reason #2: God Makes Sense of the Complexity of the Universe

"Scientists have been stunned," Craig declared, "to discover that the Big Bang was not some chaotic, primordial event, but rather a highly ordered event that required an enormous amount of information . . . [The universe] had to be fine-tuned to an incomprehensible precision for the existence of life like ourselves. That points in a very compelling way toward the existence of an Intelligent Designer."

Reason #3: God Makes Sense of Objective Moral Values

"A third factor," Craig explained, "is the existence of objective moral values. If God does not

exist, then objective moral values do not exist. Then morality is just a matter of personal taste . . . to say that killing innocent children is wrong would just be an expression of taste . . . But we all know deep down that objective moral values do exist," he continued, "so it follows logically and inescapably that God exists."

Reason #4: God Makes Sense of the Resurrection

Craig summed up this argument simply: "If Jesus of Nazareth really did come back from the dead, then we have a divine miracle on our hands and, thus, further evidence for the existence of God." This, by the way, was the primary argument that convinced me when I was a skeptic.

Reason #5: God Can Immediately Be Experienced

This last point, Craig explained, is not so much an argument as a "claim that you can know that God exists wholly apart from arguments by having an immediate experience of Him." This has certainly been true in my life, and perhaps in yours too.

The scientifically supported evidence from the origin of the universe, the fine-tuning of the universe to support life, the inescapable existence of objective moral values that originate from beyond us, the historical evidence for the resurrection of Jesus, and our own experience with the living Savior—these combine to form a powerful case for the existence of God.

> For since the creation of the world God's
> invisible qualities—his eternal power and
> divine nature—have been clearly seen,
> being understood from what has been
> made, so that people are without excuse.

ROMANS 1:20

6

How does the Big Bang theory help prove that there's a God?

For centuries philosophers have presented various forms of the "Cosmological Argument" for the existence of God—that is, arguments related to the origin and existence of the cosmos, or universe. A version called the *Kalam* argument has been championed in recent years by Dr. William Lane Craig:

- First, whatever begins to exist has a cause.
- Second, the universe began to exist.
- Therefore, the universe has a cause.

Few people argue with the first premise. In fact, science is built on the assumption that effects have a cause. The second premise, however, was once highly disputed. Secular scientists argued that the universe was eternal, without a beginning. But more recent evidence for the Big Bang shows

that everything in the physical universe came into existence in one grand cosmic explosion.

I know it sounds like science fiction. But here's what physicist and best-selling author Stephen Hawking concluded about it: "Almost everyone now believes that the universe, and time itself, had a beginning at the big bang."[4]

As Dr. Craig explained in *The Case for Faith*: "That's where the overwhelming scientific evidence points . . . [but] this poses a major problem for skeptics . . . [who] believe that the universe came from nothing and by nothing." He added with a chuckle, "Something coming from nothing makes no sense! If there must be a cause for a little bang, then doesn't it also make sense that there would be a cause for a big bang?"[5]

I think it does make sense, and that it points powerfully to the same conclusion as the opening verse in the Bible:

In the beginning God created
the heavens and the earth.

GENESIS 1:1

7

How does the beginning of the universe point specifically to the God of the Bible?

The event surrounding the beginning of the universe—the Big Bang—tells us quite a bit about the Creator. "There are several qualities we can identify," Dr. William Lane Craig explained in *The Case for a Creator*. "The cause of space and time must be an uncaused, beginningless, timeless, spaceless, immaterial, personal being endowed with freedom of will and enormous power," he said. "And that is the core concept of God."[6]

Astronomer Robert Jastrow elaborated. "The essential element in the astronomical and biblical accounts of Genesis is the same," he explains. "The chain of events leading to man commenced suddenly and sharply, at a definite moment in time, in a flash of light and energy."[7]

My colleague Mark Mittelberg summed up the argument in his book *Confident Faith*:

> But that leaves us with the realization that something *outside of the universe* caused it. That "something" would have to be big enough, smart enough, powerful enough, and old enough—not to mention have enough of a creative, artistic flair—to be able to pull off such a grand "effect." That sounds suspiciously similar to the divine being described in the book of Genesis, which starts with these words: "In the beginning God created the heavens and the earth."
>
> Or, as Robert Jastrow puts it famously at the end of *God and the Astronomers*, "For the scientist who has lived by his faith in the power of reason, the story ends like a bad dream. He has scaled the mountains of ignorance; he is about to conquer the highest peak; as he pulls himself over the final rock, he is greeted by a band of theologians who have been sitting there for centuries."[8]

The evidence related to the Big Bang doesn't tell us everything, but it tells us quite a bit about the cause behind the universe—a Cause whose characteristics correspond uncannily to the God of Scripture.

"This is what the LORD says—
your Redeemer, who formed you in the womb:
I am the LORD,
the Maker of all things,
who stretches out the heavens,
who spreads out the earth by myself."

ISAIAH 44:24

8

What is the "fine-tuning" of the universe—and what can it tell us?

One of the most striking discoveries of modern science has been that the laws and constants of physics unexpectedly conspire in extraordinary ways to make the universe suitable for life. Put another way, about fifty different factors had to be dialed in with incredible precision in order for life of any kind to survive. If even one of these areas had been off to even the slightest degree then, well, we wouldn't have been around to know about it!

But how did these factors get so dialed in? By chance? The odds against that are absolutely astronomical.

In our interview for *The Case for a Creator*, physicist Robin Collins gave an example of just one

of these areas, the cosmological constant, which represents the energy density of empty space.

"There's no way we can really comprehend it," he explained. "The fine-tuning has conservatively been estimated to be at least one part in a hundred million billion billion billion billion billion. That would be a ten followed by fifty-three zeroes. That's inconceivably precise."[9]

I couldn't imagine a figure like that. "Can you give me an illustration?"

"Let's say you were way out in space and were going to throw a dart at random toward the Earth. It would be like successfully hitting a bull's eye that's one trillionth of a trillionth of an inch in diameter. That's less than the size of one solitary atom."[10]

Breathtaking was the word that came to mind. This—just one of about fifty examples—pointed convincingly to a divine "Fine-tuner."[11] The evidence is so powerful, in fact, that it was instrumental in helping Harvard-educated professor Patrick Glynn, a spiritual skeptic, abandon his

agnosticism. And it is compelling information we can share with our friends too.

> Who has measured the waters in the hollow
>   of his hand,
> or with the breadth of his hand marked off
>   the heavens?
> Who has held the dust of the earth in a
>   basket,
> or weighed the mountains on the scales and
>   the hills in a balance?
> Who can fathom the Spirit of the LORD?
>
> ISAIAH 40:12–13

9

What are "molecular machines"— and how do they relate to discussions about God?

This may sound like something from a *Star Trek* movie, but it's actually an important topic— and one that exposes holes in current theories of evolution. It all starts with a *mousetrap*—but let's get some background first!

In our interview for *The Case for a Creator*, Dr. Michael Behe, a professor of biochemistry and author of *Darwin's Black Box*, told me about a test that Charles Darwin proposed for his own theory.

"Darwin said, 'If it could be demonstrated that any complex organ existed which could not possibly have been formed by numerous, successive, slight modifications, my theory would absolutely break down.' And that was the basis for my concept of *irreducible complexity*.

"You see, a system or device is irreducibly complex if it has a number of different components that all work together to accomplish the task of the system, and if you were to remove one of the components, the system would no longer function. An irreducibly complex system is highly unlikely to be built piece-by-piece through Darwinian processes, because the system has to be fully present in order for it to function. The illustration I like to use is a mousetrap."

I chuckled. "Do you have problems with mice at your house?"

"Actually, yes, we do," he said with a laugh. "But a mousetrap has turned out to be a great example."

Behe held up a run-of-the-mill wooden mousetrap. "You can see the interdependence of the parts for yourself," he said, pointing to each of the five components as he described them. "Now, if you take away any of these parts—the spring or the holding bar or whatever—then it's not like the mousetrap becomes half as efficient as it used to

be. It doesn't catch half as many mice. It doesn't work at all.

"So the mousetrap does a good job of illustrating how irreducibly complex biological systems defy a Darwinian explanation," he continued. "Evolution can't produce an irreducibly complex biological machine suddenly, all at once, because it's much too complicated. The odds against that would be prohibitive. And you can't produce it directly by numerous, successive, slight modifications of a precursor system, because any precursor system would be missing a part and consequently couldn't function. There would be no reason for it to exist."

I asked, "Are there a lot of different kinds of biological machines at the cellular level?"

"Life is actually based on molecular machines," he replied. "They haul cargo from one place in the cell to another; they turn cellular switches on and off; they act as pulleys and cables; electrical machines let current flow through nerves; manufacturing machines build other machines;

solar-powered machines capture the energy from light and store it in chemicals. Molecular machinery lets cells move, reproduce, and process food. In fact, every part of the cell's function is controlled by complex, highly calibrated machines."

Behe motioned toward the mousetrap. "And if the creation of a simple device like this requires intelligent design," he said, "then we have to ask, 'What about the finely tuned machines of the cellular world?' If evolution can't adequately explain them, then scientists should be free to consider other alternatives."

Behe had taken Darwin at his word and demonstrated how these interconnected biological systems could not have been created through the numerous, successive, slight modifications that his theory demands.

Behe pointed out that there is an alternative that does explain how complex biological machines could have been created. "My conclusion can be summed up in a single word: *design*," Behe said. "I say that based on science. I believe that

irreducibly complex systems are strong evidence of a purposeful, intentional design by an intelligent agent. No other theory succeeds; certainly not Darwinism."[12]

I couldn't have said it better myself!

All things have been created through
him and for him. He is before all things,
and in him all things hold together.

Colossians 1:16–17

10

Why is DNA referred to as "the language of God"— what does that mean?

As scientists have studied the six feet of DNA that's tightly coiled inside each of our body's 100 trillion cells, they have marveled at how it provides the genetic information necessary to create all of the proteins out of which our bodies are built.

The astounding capacity of DNA to harbor this mountain of information, carefully spelled out in a four-letter chemical alphabet, "vastly exceeds that of any other known system," said biochemist Michael Denton.[13]

In fact, he said the information needed to build the proteins for all the species of organisms that have ever lived "could be held in a teaspoon and

there would still be room left for all the information in every book ever written."[14]

It seemed fitting when scientists announced they had finally mapped the three billion-letter code of the human genome—a project that filled the equivalent of 75,490 pages of the *New York Times*—references to the divine abounded. President Clinton said scientists were "learning the language in which God created life," while geneticist Francis S. Collins, head of the Human Genome Project, said DNA was "our own instruction book, previously known only to God."[15]

Dr. Stephen Meyer, author of *Signature in the Cell*, concurs. He told me, "Information is the hallmark of mind. And purely from the evidence of genetics and biology, we can infer the existence of a mind that's far greater than our own—a conscious, purposeful, rational, intelligent designer who's amazingly creative."[16]

This conclusion is compelling: an intelligent entity has spelled out evidence of his existence through the chemical letters used in the genetic

code. It's almost as if, as Meyer's book title suggests, the Creator autographed every cell.

> For you created my inmost being;
> you knit me together in my mother's womb.
>> I praise you because I am fearfully and
>> wonderfully made.
>
> PSALM 139:13–14

11

Did evolution put God out of a job?

In many people's minds, evolution tells us everything we need to know about our origins—so who needs God?

Not so fast. Besides the many problems with Darwin's theory itself, there are several critical factors related to our existence that the theory doesn't even address. My colleague Mark Mittelberg listed some of these in his book, *The Questions Christians Hope No One Will Ask*.[17] He called this the "Even If" approach, meaning even if Darwin *had* been right, his theory couldn't have gotten off the ground without three essential preconditions—all of which point to intelligent design:

1. The formation of the universe itself, which Darwin's theory assumes but doesn't account for. But how did it get here, and how do

we account for its incredible life-friendly design?

2. The origin of the first life—which, again, Darwin's theory simply presupposes. In spite of his book's title, *The Origin of Species*, Darwin doesn't answer the question of where the *original* species came from.

I asked Dr. Walter Bradley, coauthor of *The Mystery of Life's Origin*, why Darwin ignored this. "Well," he answered, "he didn't really have a good idea of how life arose."[18] Even today scientists don't have a credible naturalistic theory of how life began.

3. The encoding of information in the cell— which makes all organic life possible. This, of course, relates to the discussion we had earlier about the amazingly complex information in DNA—a topic nobody in Darwin's day knew about.

The formation of the universe, the origin of the first life, the encoding of information in the

cell—these all point powerfully toward a Creator—
one whose job remains securely intact!

> Lift up your eyes and look to the heavens:
> Who created all these?
> He who brings out the starry host one by one
>   and calls forth each of them by name.

ISAIAH 40:26

12

Can you summarize what science tells us about God?

The breadth of what we can learn from the scientific data is remarkable. Here's a distillation of information from my book *The Case for a Creator*.

First, as I discussed earlier, the cause behind the beginning of the universe must be an *uncaused, timeless, immaterial, personal being* endowed with *freedom of will* and *enormous power*.

Next, the fine-tuning of the universe shows that the Creator is *intelligent* and *loving* in how he fitted our environment for life.

Also, we see from the complexity of molecular machines as well as the information encoded in DNA that the one behind life is incredibly *creative*. From just these examples, the portrait of the Creator from the scientific data is remarkably in line with the God of the Bible:

- Creator? "In the beginning you laid the foundation of the earth, and the heavens are the work of your hands" (Ps. 102:25).
- Uncaused and timeless? "Before the mountains were born or you brought forth the earth and the world, from everlasting to everlasting you are God" (Ps. 90:2).
- Immaterial? "God is spirit . . ." (John 4:24).
- Personal? "I am God Almighty" (Gen. 17:1).
- Freedom of will? "And God said, 'Let there be light,' and there was light" (Gen. 1:3).
- Enormously powerful? "The LORD is . . . great in power" (Nahum 1:3).
- Intelligent? "How many are your works, O LORD! In wisdom you made them all; the earth is full of your creatures" (Ps. 104:24).
- Loving? "The earth is full of his unfailing love" (Ps. 33:5).
- Creative? "I praise you because I am fearfully and wonderfully made; your works are wonderful, I know that full well" (Ps. 139:14).

Science doesn't tell us everything we need to know, but this much is clear: the kind of Creator science points to is one who could communicate with his creatures if he wanted to. That's why the next section will discuss questions related to what I believe to be God's revelation, the Bible.

> Many, LORD my God,
> are the wonders you have done,
> the things you planned for us.
> None can compare with you;
> were I to speak and tell of your deeds,
> they would be too many to declare.
>
> PSALM 40:5

III

Answers About the Bible

13

If the Bible was written by ordinary people, how can I know it really is the Word of God?

Yes, the authors were ordinary human beings. And what they wrote reflected their own backgrounds, experiences, and particular ways of

speaking. But, *no*, their process of writing the Bible was anything but ordinary. Here's how Peter—the disciple-turned-apostle of Jesus—described this remarkable process in 2 Peter 1:20–21:

> Above all, you must understand that no prophecy of Scripture came about by the prophet's own interpretation of things. For prophecy never had its origin in the human will, but prophets, though human, spoke from God as they were carried along by the Holy Spirit.

What Peter describes is a divine-human partnership in which God initiates and guides the process of communicating the exact message he wants to reveal. He does this through chosen prophets and apostles who accurately record that message, but in ways that reflect their own unique personalities. Also, God superintends this process so as to prevent the introduction of errors into their writings, as these verses make clear (emphases mine):

"The grass withers and the flowers fall,
but *the word of our God endures forever.*"
(Isa. 40:8)

"For truly I tell you, until heaven and earth disappear, *not the smallest letter, not the least stroke of a pen, will by any means disappear from the Law* until everything is accomplished" (Jesus, in Matt. 5:18).

"Heaven and earth will pass away, but *my words will never pass away*" (Jesus, in Luke 21:33).

"*Your word is truth*" (Jesus, talking to the Father, in John 17:17).

So in the end you're reading, for example, a psalm of David, the gospel of Luke, or a letter from Paul, but each of these can also be described as Scripture and the Word of God (2 Peter 3:16). It is truth revealed by God—and confirmed through other means, such as history and archaeology, as we'll see in other answers.

We also have the prophetic message
as something completely reliable,
and you will do well to pay attention
to it, as to a light shining in a dark
place, until the day dawns and the
morning star rises in your hearts.

2 Peter 1:19

14

Stories about Jesus were passed along verbally before being written down. How can we be sure the gospels are reliable?

I was able to sit down with New Testament scholar Craig Blomberg and ask him questions like this one. I repeated the often-heard charge that the gospels were written so far after the events that legend developed and hopelessly polluted and distorted what was finally recorded. "Is that a reasonable hypothesis?" I asked.

Blomberg was adamant. "There's good evidence for suggesting early dates for the writing of the gospels. But even if there wasn't, this argument doesn't work."

"Why not?" I asked.

"The standard scholarly dating, even in very liberal circles, is Mark in the 70s AD, Matthew

and Luke in the 80s AD, John in the 90s AD. [Jesus was executed in AD 30 or 33.] But that's still within the lifetimes of eyewitnesses of the life of Jesus, including hostile eyewitnesses who would have served as a corrective if false teachings about Jesus were going around. Consequently, these late dates for the gospels really aren't all that late."[1]

In fact, one of the greatest classical historians, A. N. Sherwin-White of Oxford University, understood the rate at which legend developed in the ancient world. He said that the passage of two generations of time was not even enough for legend to develop and wipe out a solid core of historical truth.[2]

I reflected on modern events that happened about thirty to sixty years ago. The presidency of Ronald Reagan, the assassination of President Kennedy, the Vietnam War, even the Korean War—there are plenty of eyewitnesses around today who have detailed memories of these. How much more would the writers of the gospels recall

the words and deeds of the one they knew to be God's Son?

> "The Holy Spirit, whom the Father will send in my name, will teach you all things and will remind you of everything I have said to you."

> JESUS, IN JOHN 14:26

15

How soon after Jesus' death were the gospels written?

It seems obvious that the shorter the gap between an event and when it is written down, the less likely those writings will fall victim to faulty memories or legend. So this question is an important one.

Although the standard scholarly dating of the Gospels is in the 70s AD, 80s AD, and 90s AD, Dr. Craig Blomberg said earlier dates can be supported by looking at the book of Acts, which was written by Luke, a physician, historian, and close companion of the apostle Paul.

"Acts ends apparently unfinished—Paul is a central figure of the book, and he's under house arrest in Rome. With that the book abruptly halts," said Blomberg, who is the author of *The*

Historical Reliability of the Gospels. "What happens to Paul? We don't find out from Acts, probably because the book was written before Paul was put to death.

"That means Acts cannot be dated any later than AD 62. Having established that, we can then move backward from there. Since Acts is the second of a two-part work, we know the first part—the gospel of Luke—must have been written earlier than that. And since Luke incorporates parts of the gospel of Mark, this means Mark is even earlier.

"If you allow maybe a year for each of those, you end up with Mark written no later than about AD 60, maybe even the late 50s. If Jesus was put to death in AD 30 or 33, we're talking about a maximum gap of thirty years or so."

He sat back in his chair with an air of triumph. "Historically speaking," he said, "that's like a news flash!"[3]

That *was* impressive, closing the gap between the events of Jesus' life and the writing of the

Gospels to the point where it seemed that serious errors were unlikely.

That which was from the beginning,
which we have heard, which we have seen
with our eyes, which we have looked at
and our hands have touched—this we
proclaim concerning the Word of life.

1 JOHN 1:1

16

I've heard people say the New Testament borrowed themes of dying and rising gods from earlier mythical religions. Is there any truth to this?

This is one of the most prevalent claims on the Internet: Christianity is a copycat religion that stole its essential beliefs from earlier myths. In other words, the resurrection of Jesus never really happened—it was merely a story that Christians plagiarized from ancient mythology.

This idea was popularized by *The Da Vinci Code*, which declared, "Nothing in Christianity is original."[4] For instance, proponents of this theory will tell you there were stories of an earlier mythological god named Mithras long before Jesus was born. They say Mithras was born of a virgin in a cave on December 25, was considered a great

traveling teacher, had twelve disciples, sacrificed himself for world peace, was buried in a tomb, and rose again three days later.

Sound familiar? This seems to prove that Christianity merely stole its ideas about Jesus from the mystery religion called Mithraism. But what do we find when we look at the story a bit more carefully?

- Mithras was born of a virgin in a cave? **No, actually the myth says Mithras emerged fully grown out of a rock! No virgins and no caves. Besides, nowhere does the Bible say that Jesus was born in a cave.**
- Mithras was born on December 25? **Okay, but so what? The Bible doesn't say when Jesus was born. Some think it was in the spring, others in January. It wasn't until centuries later that Christians chose December 25 as the date to celebrate his birth—in part to claim a pagan holiday for Christ.**
- Mithras was a traveling teacher with twelve disciples? **No, he was supposedly a god, not**

a teacher, and in the Iranian version of the story he had just one follower, while in the Roman version he had two followers—but never twelve.

- Mithras sacrificed himself for world peace? No, actually he was known for killing a bull. He didn't sacrifice himself for anything.
- Mithras was buried in a tomb and resurrected after three days? No, we have absolutely no record of any beliefs about the death of Mithras, and there was therefore no resurrection either.

So look what happened—the parallels between Mithras and Jesus evaporated under cross-examination.

Here's the truth, as summarized by a senior Swedish scholar in a recent academic treatise:[5] the nearly universal consensus of scholars is that there are no examples of any mythological gods dying and rising from the dead that came before Jesus. These resurrection myths came *after* Christianity. So if anyone stole any ideas, it was

the mythical religions borrowing from the truths of Christianity!

There's a broader principle worth noting. The Bible tells us in 1 Thessalonians 5:21 to test truth claims, and to "hold on to what is good." How can we do this? By looking at both sides of the story and weighing the evidence carefully. As Proverbs 18:17 explains, "In a lawsuit the first to speak seems right, until someone comes forward and cross-examines."

So never be afraid to step forward and cross-examine—and always stay eager to "hold on to what is good."

> For we did not follow cleverly devised myths when we made known to you the power and coming of our Lord Jesus Christ, but we were eyewitnesses of his majesty.
>
> 2 PETER 1:16 ESV

17

Who decided which books made
it into the New Testament and
which ones didn't? How do
we know they got it right?

This is a question about the New Testament *canon*, a term that describes which books have been accepted as official and are therefore included in the Bible. I raised this issue with renowned New Testament scholar Bruce Metzger when I interviewed him for *The Case for Christ*.

"How did the early church leaders determine which books would be considered authoritative and which would be discarded?" I asked. "And what criteria did they use in determining which documents would be included in the New Testament?"

"Basically, the early church had three criteria," he said. "First, the books must have apostolic

authority—that is, they must have been written either by apostles themselves, who were eyewitnesses to what they wrote about, or by followers of apostles.

"Second, there was the criterion of conformity to what was called the rule of faith. That is, was the document congruent with the basic Christian tradition that the church recognized as normative?

"And third, there was the criterion of whether a document had had continuous acceptance and usage by the church at large.

"What's remarkable," Metzger continued, "is that even though the fringes of the canon remained unsettled for a while, there was actually a high degree of unanimity concerning the greater part of the New Testament within the first two centuries. And this was true among very diverse congregations scattered over a wide area."[6]

Another authority in this area, F. F. Bruce, added in his book *The New Testament Documents: Are They Reliable?* "The historic Christian belief is that the Holy Spirit, who controlled the writing of the individual books, also controlled their

selection and collection, thus continuing to fulfill our Lord's promise that he would guide his
disciples 'into all the truth' (John 16:13)."[7]

So we can see there was both divine and
human care in collecting the canon of books that
we now know as the New Testament Scriptures.

All Scripture is God-breathed and is
useful for teaching, rebuking, correcting
and training in righteousness, so that
the servant of God may be thoroughly
equipped for every good work.

2 Timothy 3:16–17

18

What are the gnostic gospels—and why were they excluded from the Bible?

There have been many claims surrounding the "gnostic gospels." In fact, the theologically liberal scholars who comprise the ironically named Jesus Seminar published *The Complete Gospels*, presenting sixteen other so-called gospels alongside Matthew, Mark, Luke, and John—suggesting they're equally valid.

But are they? Not even close, scholar Bruce Metzger told me. "They're written later than the four gospels, in the second, third, fourth, fifth, even sixth century, long after Jesus, and they're generally quite banal. They carry names—like the Gospel of Peter and the Gospel of Mary—that are unrelated to their real authorship."[8]

Even the earliest examples like the Gospel

of Thomas and the Gospel of Judas were written between AD 175 and 200—more than 140 years after the life of Jesus. Who do you think would be the more accurate in writing the story of Abraham Lincoln: someone who lived in the same time frame and was able to draw from eyewitness accounts of his life, or someone today who's relying on stories and rumors that have floated down through almost a century and a half of time? The answer is obvious.

In addition, there are troublesome teachings in these so-called gospels. N. T. Wright says in *Judas and the Gospel of Jesus* that the gnostics historically held four basic ideas: "a wicked world; a wicked god who made it; salvation consisting of rescue from it; and rescue coming through the imparting of secret knowledge, especially knowledge that one has the divine spark within one's own self."[9] Even a cursory reading of the biblical gospels shows these ideas are alien to Jesus' teachings. For example, in them he explains that God is good (Luke 18:19), that he wants us to be an influence in the world—not to be plucked out of

it (John 17:15), and that salvation comes not from secret knowledge but from knowing the true God (John 17:3).

Bottom line: No other accounts about Jesus pass the test the way Matthew, Mark, Luke, and John do. We can trust the four gospels because they were written close to the life of Jesus, they're rooted in eyewitness testimony, they're corroborated in key places by history and archaeology, and they square with other biblical teachings—none of which is true of the gnostic gospels.

> We proclaim to you what we have
> seen and heard, so that you also
> may have fellowship with us.

1 JOHN 1:3

19

I keep hearing people mention the Gospel of Thomas. Is it worth studying?

The Gospel of Thomas is, by far, the most prominent of the gnostic gospels, which were discussed in answer 18—and its proponents claim it is as reliable as Matthew, Mark, Luke, and John in the New Testament.

However, the biblical gospels were written in the first century, whereas the Gospel of Thomas was written, at the earliest, about a hundred years later—in the late second century. So it was much further removed from Jesus' life.

Worse, its teachings run the gamut from unbiblical to illogical. For example, Thomas proclaims that salvation comes from understanding oneself authentically—a message diametrically opposed to the biblical gospel. It also claims Jesus said, "If

you fast, you will bring sin upon yourselves, and if you pray, you will be condemned, and if you give to charity, you will harm your spirits."[10]

It gets even worse. Thomas quotes Jesus as saying, "Lucky is the lion that the human will eat, so that the lion becomes human. And foul is the human that the lion will eat, and the lion still will become human."[11] *Huh?*

In addition, Thomas portrays Jesus as anti-women. At one point, Simon Peter says to him, "Make Mary leave us, for females don't deserve life." Jesus allegedly responds, "Look, I will guide her to make her male, so she too may become a living spirit resembling you males. For every female who makes herself male will enter the domain of Heaven."[12]

This is obviously in sharp contrast to the teachings of the real Jesus, who elevated women in a very countercultural way.

For these reasons and more, I'm a doubting Thomas regarding the Gospel of Thomas—and I'm confident the real Thomas, the authentic one in

the New Testament gospels, would have doubted and rejected it as well!

> Since I myself have carefully investigated
> everything from the beginning, I too
> decided to write an orderly account for
> you . . . so that you may know the certainty
> of the things you have been taught.

LUKE 1:3–4

20

Were there really ancient prophecies predicting details about the life and ministry of Jesus?

The Old Testament contains numerous predictions about the coming Messiah, and when you piece them all together they create a "fingerprint" of who he would be and what he would do. The Bible teaches that we can have absolute confidence that whoever fits this fingerprint is truly the Messiah—and of all the people who ever walked the earth, only Jesus Christ matches it.

In *The Case for Christ,* I interviewed Louis Lapides, a Jewish man who encountered these prophecies years ago. "I was reading the Old Testament every day and seeing one prophecy after another," he said. "For instance, Deuteronomy talked about a prophet greater than Moses who will come and whom we should listen to. I thought,

Who can be greater than Moses? It sounded like the Messiah—someone as great and respected as Moses but a greater teacher and a greater authority. I grabbed ahold of that and went searching for him."[13]

As Lapides progressed through the Scriptures, he was stopped cold by Isaiah 53. With clarity and specificity, in a haunting prediction wrapped in exquisite poetry, here was the picture of a Messiah who would suffer and die for the sins of Israel and the world—all written more than seven hundred years before Jesus walked the earth.

> He was despised and rejected by men,
> a man of sorrows, and familiar with
> suffering.
> Like one from whom men hide their faces
> he was despised, and we esteemed him
> not.
> Surely he took up our infirmities
> and carried our sorrows,
> yet we considered him stricken by God,
> smitten by him, and afflicted.

But he was pierced for our transgressions,
    he was crushed for our iniquities;
the punishment that brought us peace was
   upon him,
    and by his wounds we are healed.
We all, like sheep, have gone astray,
    each of us has turned to his own way;
and the Lord has laid on him
    the iniquity of us all . . .
For he bore the sin of many,
and made intercession for the transgressors.

Isaiah 53:3–6, 12

Instantly Lapides recognized this as a portrait of Jesus of Nazareth! He began to understand the paintings he had seen as a child: the suffering Jesus, the crucified Jesus, the Jesus who had been "pierced for our transgressions" as he "bore the sin of many."

Over and over Lapides would come upon prophecies in the Old Testament—more than four dozen major predictions in all. Isaiah revealed the manner of the Messiah's birth (of a virgin, Isaiah

7:14); Micah pinpointed the place of his birth (Bethlehem, Micah 5:2); Genesis and Jeremiah specified his ancestry (a descendent of Abraham, Isaac, and Jacob, from the tribe of Judah, the house of David, Genesis 21:12, 49:8–12, Jeremiah 23:5–6); the Psalms foretold his betrayal, his accusation by false witnesses, his manner of death (pierced in the hands and feet, although crucifixion hadn't even been invented yet, Psalm 22); and his resurrection (he would not decay but would ascend on high, Psalm 16:10); and on and on. Each one chipped away at Lapides's skepticism about Jesus, until he was finally willing to take a drastic step.

One night in the Mojave Desert he cried out, "God, I've got to come to the end of this struggle. I have to know beyond a shadow of a doubt that Jesus is the Messiah. I need to know that you, as the God of Israel, want me to believe this."[14]

God gave Lapides the certainty he was looking for, so he received the forgiveness and leadership of Christ and began following him from that time forward. He later married Deborah, another Jewish follower of Jesus, and together they

founded a fellowship of Jewish and Gentile believers where he served as the pastor for many years.

The Messianic prophecies played a huge role in leading Lapides to faith in Christ, and they were compelling to me when I encountered them as a skeptic—as they still are today.

> "This is what I told you while I was still with you: Everything must be fulfilled that is written about me in the Law of Moses, the Prophets and the Psalms."

JESUS, AFTER HIS RESURRECTION, IN LUKE 24:44

21

Couldn't someone other than Jesus, past or future, fulfill the prophecies and fit the "fingerprint" of the Messiah?

In *The Case for the Real Jesus,* I interviewed Dr. Michael Brown, a Jewish scholar and follower of Jesus. He explained why Jesus—and Jesus alone—fits the fingerprint of the prophecies about the Messiah.

"In 2 Chronicles 7, God says if Israel's sin reaches a certain level, he'll destroy the temple, exile the people, and leave them in a state of judgment," Brown said. "Sure enough, this comes to pass. The prophet Daniel prays in Daniel 9 that God would have mercy. God gives him a revelation about the temple being rebuilt. Before this new temple is destroyed, Daniel is told, several things are going to take place, including the

bringing of everlasting atonement—the final dealing with sin."

He continued, "the prophet Haggai said the glory of the second temple would be greater than the glory of the first temple. God would fill the second temple with his glory. Then the prophet Malachi said the Lord will come to his temple. He uses a Hebrew term that always refers to God himself: the Lord—he will come to that temple.

"Keep in mind the second temple was destroyed in AD 70. *Atonement for sin had to be made and the divine visitation had to take place before the second temple was destroyed.*

"So . . . if it's not Yeshua, which is the Jewish name for Jesus, then throw out the Bible," Brown concluded, "because nobody except him accomplished what needed to be done prior to AD 70. What divine visitation *did* take place if not for Yeshua? When else *did* God visit the second temple in a personal way? Who else atoned for sin? How else *was* the glory of the second temple greater than the first?

"Either the Messiah came two thousand years

ago or the prophets were wrong and we can discard the Bible. But they weren't wrong. Yeshua is the Messiah—or nobody is."[15]

> But when the set time had fully come, God
> sent his Son, born of a woman, born under
> the law, to redeem those under the law,
> that we might receive adoption to sonship.
>
> GALATIANS 4:4–5

22

Is there any historical evidence from outside the Bible to show it is true?

There are many outside sources that corroborate the claims of the Bible. Dr. Gary Habermas, in *The Historical Jesus*, details thirty-nine ancient sources documenting the life of Jesus, from which he enumerates more than one hundred reported facts concerning Jesus' life, teachings, crucifixion, and resurrection.[16]

What's more, twenty-four of the sources cited by Habermas, including seven secular sources and several of the earliest creeds of the church, specifically concern the divine nature of Jesus. "These creeds reveal that the church did not simply teach Jesus' deity a generation later . . . this doctrine is definitely present in the earliest church," said the historian.[17]

Professor Edwin Yamauchi adds, "When people begin religious movements, it's often not until many generations later that people record things about them, but the fact is that we have better historical documentation for Jesus than for the founder of any other ancient religion . . . [it's] quite impressive in terms of how much we can learn about him aside from the New Testament."[18]

I asked Dr. Yamauchi what we could conclude about Jesus from ancient non-Christian sources. "We would know that first, Jesus was a Jewish teacher; second, many people believed that he performed healings and exorcisms; third, some people believed he was the Messiah; fourth, he was rejected by the Jewish leaders; fifth, he was crucified under Pontius Pilate in the reign of Tiberius; sixth, despite this shameful death, his followers, who believed that he was still alive, spread beyond Palestine so that there were multitudes of them in Rome by AD 64; and seventh, all kinds of people from the cities and countryside—men and women, slave and free—worshiped him as God."[19]

This was indeed impressive outside corroboration for the claims of the New Testament—and more reasons we can have a confident faith in Christ.

> Jesus did many other things as well. If every one of them were written down, I suppose that even the whole world would not have room for the books that would be written.

JOHN 21:25

23

What does archaeology tell us about the validity of the Old Testament?

I asked this question of Dr. Norman Geisler, author of more than sixty books, in my interview with him for *The Case for Faith*. His answer was characteristically confident and compelling.

"There have been thousands of archaeological finds in the Middle East that support the picture presented in the biblical record," Geisler began. "There was a discovery not long ago confirming King David. The patriarchs—the narratives about Abraham, Isaac, and Jacob—were once considered legendary, but as more has become known, these stories are increasingly corroborated. The destruction of Sodom and Gomorrah was thought to be mythological until evidence was uncovered that all five of the cities mentioned in Genesis

were, in fact, situated just as the Old Testament said. As far as their destruction goes, archaeologist Clifford Wilson said there is 'permanent evidence of the great conflagration that took place in the long distant past.'[20]

"Furthermore," Geisler added, "various aspects of the Jewish captivity have been confirmed. Also, every reference in the Old Testament to an Assyrian king has been proven correct; an excavation during the 1960s confirmed that the Israelites could, indeed, have entered Jerusalem by way of a tunnel during David's reign; there is evidence the world did have a single language at one time, as the Bible says; the site of Solomon's temple is now being excavated; and on and on. Many times, archaeologists have been skeptical of the Old Testament, only to have new discoveries corroborate the biblical account."

"For example? " I asked.

"The Bible makes about three dozen references to the Hittites, but critics used to charge that there was no evidence that such people ever existed. Now archaeologists digging in modern Turkey

have discovered the records of the Hittites. As the great archaeologist William F. Albright declared, 'There can be no doubt that archaeology has confirmed the substantial historicity of the Old Testament tradition.'"[21]

Suffice it to say: while not everything in the Old Testament can be tested by archaeology, discoveries have repeatedly confirmed claims made by these Scriptures.

> "For what god is there in heaven
> or on earth who can do the deeds
> and mighty works you do?"

D E U T E R O N O M Y 3:24

24

Does archaeology confirm the New Testament?

In my interview with Dr. Norman Geisler, I asked him to briefly summarize the archaeological evidence supporting the New Testament.

"The noted Roman historian Colin J. Hemer, in *The Book of Acts in the Setting of Hellenistic History*, shows how archaeology has confirmed not dozens, but hundreds and hundreds of details from the biblical account of the early church,"[22] Geisler said. "Even small details have been corroborated, like which way the wind blows, how deep the water is a certain distance from the shore, what kind of disease a particular island had, the names of local officials, and so forth.

"Now, Acts was authored by the historian Luke. Hemer gives more than a dozen reasons

why Acts had to have been written before AD 62, or about thirty years after Jesus' crucifixion. Even earlier, Luke wrote the gospel of Luke, which is substantially the same as the other biblical accounts of Jesus' life.

"So here you have an impeccable historian, who has been proven right in hundreds of details and never proven wrong, writing the whole history of Jesus and the early church. And it's written within one generation while eyewitnesses were still alive and could have disputed it if it were exaggerated or false. You don't have anything like that from any other religious book from the ancient world."

"Is Hemer a lone voice on that?" I asked.

"Hardly," Geisler replied. "Prominent historian Sir William Ramsay started out as a skeptic, but after studying Acts he concluded that 'in various details the narrative showed marvelous truth.'[23] The great Oxford University classical historian A. N. Sherwin-White said, 'For Acts the confirmation of historicity is overwhelming,'

and that 'any attempt to reject its basic historicity must now appear absurd.'"[24]

"I have spoken to you of earthly things
and you do not believe; how then will you
believe if I speak of heavenly things?"

JESUS, IN JOHN 3:12

25

Doesn't the Bible contradict what we've learned from science?

This might surprise you: most of the battles happening today are not between science and the Bible—they're between *science and science*!

Or, perhaps more accurately, the conflict is between various *philosophies* of science. Specifically, there is a war raging between those who try to hold science hostage to naturalistic causes only (as opposed to considering supernatural causes) and those who want to stay open to any and all causes indicated by the evidence (including the supernatural). All too often, the first group tries to write God out of the equation even before considering the facts.

And unfortunately, this group currently has the most influence at many of our colleges and universities. This can lead to the unwarranted

conclusion that science has somehow disproven the existence of a divine being, or that thinking people simply can't take spiritual beliefs seriously. In reality, the scientific evidence for God is getting stronger and stronger, and increasing numbers of science professionals are acknowledging their belief in him.

Dr. Stephen Meyer, director of the Discovery Institute's Center for Science and Culture, is one of them. He lays out this important challenge to his colleagues: "Let's have a new period in the history of science where we actually foster the unfettered seeking of truth. Scientists should be allowed to follow the evidence wherever it leads."[25]

It sounds like common sense, doesn't it? Unfortunately, it's quite uncommon. In many schools and scientific societies, the unwritten rules say that scientists must *stop* following the evidence as soon as it starts pointing toward the supernatural.

We don't need to play by those self-imposed limitations. The Bible tells us to "love truth" (Zech. 8:19)—which must include truth that points toward *natural* as well as *supernatural* causes.

And, interestingly, the data of science have an uncanny knack for painting the same picture as the verses of the Bible.

> People . . . suppress the truth by their
> wickedness, since what may be known
> about God is plain to them, because
> God has made it plain to them.
>
> ROMANS 1:18–19

26

How can we be sure the Bible we have today is the same Bible they had back when it was written?

This question usually flows from the fact that we don't have any of the original documents of the Bible. Those crumbled into dust long ago, so how can we know the message hasn't changed? This bothered me—until I learned there are no originals left of *any* ancient literature. Instead, we have handwritten copies—manuscripts.

"What the New Testament has in its favor, especially when compared with other ancient writings, is the unprecedented multiplicity of copies that have survived," Dr. Daniel B. Wallace explained to me. "We have more witnesses to the text of the New Testament than to any other ancient Greek or Latin literature. It's really an embarrassment of riches!"

Obviously more copies means a greater chance of accuracy. "How many exist?" I asked Wallace.

"We have more than 5,700 Greek copies of the New Testament [now 5,800]. There are another 10,000 copies in Latin. Then there are versions Coptic, Syriac, Armenian, Georgian, and so on. These are estimated to number between 10,000 and 15,000. So right there we've got 25,000 to 30,000 handwritten copies of the New Testament."

I asked about the dating of the copies.

"Through the first three centuries, we have nearly fifty manuscripts in Greek alone," Wallace explained, adding that several papyri of the New Testament have been dated to the early second century—the most famous being the John Rylands fragment of the gospel of John, found in Egypt and dating to a few decades after the original.

"So we have a really small gap between the earliest papyrus and the New Testament," I summarized.

"Right. There's just no comparison to others," he said. "The average Greek author has fewer than twenty copies of his works still in existence,

and they come from no sooner than five hundred to a thousand years later."[26]

We really do have a wealth of evidence—*an embarrassment of riches*—for the New Testament, and the Old Testament has similar support. Translation: the Bible you read today is a trustworthy rendition of the original writings.

> "Heaven and earth will pass away, but
> my words will never pass away."
>
> Jesus, in Mark 13:31

27

With all the differences between the New Testament manuscripts, how can we trust the Bible?

This challenge has long been known, but has been amplified by agnostic professor Bart Ehrman in his book *Misquoting Jesus*—which was the top-selling religion book in America for many weeks.

Ehrman points out that we don't have the original copies of the New Testament.[27] That's true—though we don't have the originals of any ancient writings, sacred or secular. What we have instead are handwritten copies.

Ehrman also states correctly that there are between 200,000 and 400,000 variants, or differences, between the copies that we have.[28] So the implication is clear: How can we trust the Bible if it's pockmarked with errors? How do we really

know what the original documents said if we don't actually possess any of them?

This has shaken the faith of some people—but need not. We have good reasons to believe the New Testament has been reliably preserved for us.

First, the more copies you have of any document, the more variations you'll have. So, for example, if you only have a handful of manuscript copies—as in the case of most ancient literature—then there won't be very many differences either. But when you have over 5,800 manuscript copies of the New Testament, then you'll also have many more variations between them. So the high number of variants is actually a by-product of the overwhelming quantity of copies that we have—and is a mark of strength.

Second, the more copies you have, the easier it is to determine what the original said, because there's so much more to compare between them in order to weed out mistakes.

I should add that up to 80 percent of the variants in the New Testament documents are minor spelling errors. And only 1 percent have some

chance of affecting the meaning in some way. And even those are largely about insignificant issues—with not a single doctrine of the church in jeopardy.[29]

In the end, the New Testament has unprecedented support for its textual accuracy.

> "Blessed is the one who keeps the words
> of the prophecy written in this scroll."

JESUS, IN REVELATION 22:7

28

The Bible has been translated and retranslated so many times—and there are so many different versions—who knows what it's really supposed to say?

Some liken how we got our Bibles to the children's game of Telephone, where a message is whispered into a person's ear. Then that person whispers the message in the next person's ear, and so on around the circle. When the last individual finally says it out loud, it has become completely garbled.

The implication is that the transmission of Scripture was like this, so we can't trust that our Bibles today represent what was originally written. Dr. Daniel B. Wallace, however, told me this analogy breaks down at several key points.

"First," he said, "rather than having one stream of transmission, we have multiple streams. Now suppose you were to interrogate the last person in, say, three lines. All of them repeat the message they heard in their own line, and that message ultimately goes back to one source . . . By a little detective work, you could figure out much of what the original message was by comparing the three different reports of it.

"A second difference," he continued, "is that rather than dealing with an *oral* tradition, textual criticism deals with a *written* tradition. Now, if each person wrote down what he heard from the person in front of him, the chances for garbling the message would be remote.

"A third difference is that the textual critic— the person trying to reconstruct what the original message was—does not have to rely on that last person in the chain. He can interrogate folks who are closer to the original source."[30]

Wallace's conclusion? For these reasons and more, the process of getting the Bible wasn't anything like the game of Telephone.

And what about the many modern translations? Do they hopelessly contradict each other?
Not at all! All of the reputable translations are
based on the Greek (New Testament) and Hebrew
(Old Testament) manuscripts, and therefore say
the same thing in differing ways. That's why, for
example, BibleGateway.com can confidently dis-
play forty-five different English translations—to
let readers study the nuances in wording in order
to get a better sense of the original meaning of
Scripture.

We also have the prophetic message as
something completely reliable, and you
will do well to pay attention to it.

2 PETER 1:19

IV

Answers About Jesus

29

Was the idea of Jesus' virgin birth copied from pagan sources?

Matthew, a follower of Jesus, and Luke, who "carefully investigated everything" about Jesus, both reported that Jesus was born to a virgin.[1] Indeed, the virgin birth was foretold hundreds of years in advance in Isaiah 7:14: "Therefore

the Lord himself will give you a sign: The virgin will conceive and give birth to a son, and will call him Immanuel."

The evidence fails to support accusations that the virgin birth story was stolen from pagan religions. "Some of those [myths] that are often cited—like Zeus—are anthropomorphic gods who lust after human women, which is decidedly different from Jesus' story," historian Edwin Yamauchi explained to me.

"The mythological offspring are half gods and half men and their lives begin at conception, as opposed to Jesus, who is fully God and fully man and who is eternal but came into this world through the incarnation," Yamauchi continued. "Also, the Gospels put Jesus in a historical context, unlike the mythological gods."[2]

Even theologically liberal professor Thomas Boslooper, who wrote a book about the virgin birth, scoffed at the suggestion that the claim was derived from pagan myths:

The literature . . . which produced this conclusion and which has become the author- ity for contemporary scholars who wish to perpetuate the notion that the virgin birth in the New Testament has a non-Christian source, is characterized by brief word, phrase, and sentence quotations that have been lifted out of context or incorrectly translated and used to support preconceived theories. Sweeping generalizations based on ques- tionable evidence have become dogmatic conclusions that cannot be substantiated on the basis of careful investigation.[3]

So allegations that Christianity stole its belief about the virgin birth from pagan sources fare no better than the disproven claims that Christianity copied Jesus' resurrection from myths of dying and rising gods.

All this took place to fulfill what the Lord had said through the prophet: "The virgin will conceive and give birth to a son, and they will call him Immanuel" (which means "God with us").

30

Is there any evidence outside the Bible for the slaughter of children described in Matthew's gospel?

Matthew paints a grisly scene: Herod the Great, feeling threatened by the birth of a baby whom he feared could seize his throne, dispatches troops to Bethlehem to murder children under the age of two. Warned by an angel, Joseph escapes to Egypt with Mary and Jesus. Only after Herod dies do they return to settle in Nazareth.

Is there confirmation outside the Bible for these mass murders? No. Can we believe Matthew? Yes. Here's why:

First, the gospel of Matthew has good credentials, being based on the disciple's account and written in the first century, shortly after the events described.

Second, much of what historians wrote in the first century has been lost, so we don't know what they did or didn't report on these killings.

Third, while today an event like this slaughter would be splashed all over the news, we have to put ourselves back into the first century and keep several things in mind.

For instance, how many babies of that age would there have been in such a small village? German scholar Joseph Knabenbauer estimates fifteen or twenty.[4]

Also, Herod was notoriously bloodthirsty: he killed members of his own family and executed many people who challenged him. Murdering babies in Bethlehem would have been consistent with his character and probably would not have captivated the attention of the Roman world.

So this just wasn't considered much of an event. A madman killing everybody who might be a threat? That was business as usual under the reign of Herod. Only as Christianity developed was this incident viewed as significant.

It's worth adding that news in that day traveled slowly, if at all—especially events in such a small and seemingly insignificant village.

Consequently, in the absence of any contradictory discoveries and in light of Matthew's credibility, it's reasonable to accept his reporting as accurate.

An angel of the Lord appeared to Joseph
in a dream. "Get up," he said, "take the
child and his mother and escape to Egypt.
Stay there until I tell you, for Herod is
going to search for the child to kill him."

MATTHEW 2:13

31

Was Jesus really convinced he was the Son of God?

I asked that question of Dr. Ben Witherington III, the author of *The Christology of Jesus*, in our interview for *The Case for Christ*. Based on the evidence, Witherington replied:

> Did Jesus believe he was the Son of God, the anointed one of God? The answer is yes. Did he see himself as the Son of Man? The answer is yes. Did he see himself as the final Messiah? Yes, that's the way he viewed himself. Did he believe that anybody less than God could save the world? No, I don't believe he did.[5]

It's clear that Jesus' term for himself, "Son of God," points to his deity. This was confirmed in John 5:17 where he told the religious leaders who

were challenging him, "My Father is always at his work to this very day, and I too am working." This claim infuriated these men, because they understood what he was really saying.

In fact, John—a disciple of Jesus—summarized the situation: "For this reason they tried all the more to kill him; not only was he breaking the Sabbath, but he was even calling God his own Father, making himself equal with God" (John 5:18).

Jesus even went so far as to insist on belief in this claim—that he was the unique Son of God—as a litmus test for his followers. In Matthew 16:13–17, he asked his disciples who people thought he was. They replied, "Some say John the Baptist; others say Elijah; and still others, Jeremiah or one of the prophets."

"But what about you?" Jesus asked them. "Who do you say I am?"

Peter answered, "You are the Messiah, the Son of the living God."

Jesus replied, "Blessed are you, Simon son of Jonah, for this was not revealed to you by flesh and blood, but by my Father in heaven."

Clearly Jesus knew he was the Son of God—
and wanted us to know as well.

> "For God so loved the world that
> he gave his one and only Son, that
> whoever believes in him shall not
> perish but have eternal life."

JESUS, IN JOHN 3:16

32

Jesus called himself the "Son of Man." Doesn't this mean he was merely human?

That's a natural way to see that phrase—in fact, it's what I thought when I first encountered it. But this illustrates why it's so important to study terms in their original language and context.

Scholars have shown that Jesus' repeated references to himself as the Son of Man were actually not a claim of humanity, though he certainly was human. Rather, the phrase came from an Old Testament passage, Daniel 7:13–14, in which the Son of Man has universal authority and everlasting dominion, and receives the worship of all nations. Theologian William Lane Craig summarized, "Thus, the claim to be the Son of Man would be in effect a claim to divinity."[6]

No one would have better understood what

Jesus meant than the theologians of his day. So it's telling to see their reactions during his trial in Mark 14, where the high priest asked, "Are you the Messiah, the Son of the Blessed One?" (v. 61).

"I am," said Jesus. "And you will see the Son of Man sitting at the right hand of the Mighty One and coming on the clouds of heaven" (Mark 14:62). Jesus, in this one statement, affirmed that he was the Messiah, the Son of the Blessed One, the Son of Man, and he would one day come back.

That last part really grabbed their attention. If there was any doubt that his "Son of Man" reference alluded to the divine person described in Daniel, the "coming with the clouds of heaven," from Daniel 7:13, quickly removed it. This was a clear claim to deity!

Their reaction? "The high priest tore his clothes. 'Why do we need any more witnesses . . . You have heard the blasphemy.'" Then it says, "They all condemned him as worthy of death" (Mark 14:63–64).

Their response confirmed what Jesus meant. He was the Son of Man, the incarnation of God, the Savior of the world.

"For the Son of Man is going to come
in his Father's glory with his angels,
and then he will reward each person
according to what they have done."

JESUS, IN MATTHEW 16:27

33

Could Jesus have been crazy when he claimed to be the Son of God?

Jesus claimed to be both "the Son of God" and "the Son of Man"—both clear claims of deity. But how do we know he wasn't simply deluded? I talked about this with Dr. Gary Collins, a psychology professor and author of more than 50 books and 150 articles on a variety of psychological issues.

"It's true that people with psychological difficulties will often claim to be somebody they're not," Collins said. "However, psychologists go much deeper than that. They'll look at a person's emotions, because disturbed individuals frequently show inappropriate depression, or they might be vehemently angry, or perhaps they're plagued with anxiety. But look at Jesus: he never demonstrated inappropriate emotions.

"Deluded people will have misperceptions," he added. "They think people are trying to get them. Again, we don't see this in Jesus. He wasn't paranoid. Or people with psychological difficulties may have thinking disorders—they can't carry on a logical conversation. Jesus spoke clearly, powerfully and eloquently. He was brilliant and had absolutely amazing insights into human nature.

"He was loving but didn't let his compassion immobilize him," Collins continued. "He didn't have a bloated ego, even though he was often surrounded by adoring crowds; he maintained balance despite an often demanding lifestyle; he always knew what he was doing and where he was going; he cared deeply about people; he was able to accept people while not winking at their sin; he responded to individuals based on what they uniquely needed."

"So, Doctor—your diagnosis?" I asked.

"All in all, I just don't see signs that Jesus was suffering from any known mental illness," he

concluded, adding with a smile, "He was much healthier than anyone else I know—including me!"[7]

The Word became flesh and made
his dwelling among us. We have
seen his glory, the glory of the one
and only Son, who came from the
Father, full of grace and truth.

JOHN 1:14

34

Did Jesus' life demonstrate that he was a divine person?

While Jesus made claims to divinity in a variety of ways, it's natural to ask whether his life backed up those claims. Here's a brief summary of some of the evidence.

Biblical theologians have long taught that the primary attributes of God are *omniscience* (all-knowing), *omnipresence* (present everywhere), *omnipotence* (all power), *eternality* (always existed—and always will), and *immutability* (unchanging).

Every one of these attributes of God, says the New Testament, is found also in Jesus Christ:

- Omniscience? In John 16:30, the apostle John affirms of Jesus, "Now we can see that you know all things."

- Omnipresence? Jesus said in Matthew 28:20, "Surely I am with you always, to the very end of the age," and in Matthew 18:20, "Where two or three gather in my name, there am I with them."

- Omnipotence? "All authority in heaven and on earth has been given to me," Jesus said in Matthew 28:18.

- Eternality? John 1:1, 14 declares of Jesus, "In the beginning was the Word, and the Word was with God, and the Word was God . . . The Word became flesh and made his dwelling among us."

- Immutability? Hebrews 13:8 says, "Jesus Christ is the same yesterday and today and forever."

Also, the Old Testament paints a portrait of God by using such descriptive titles as Alpha and Omega, Lord, Savior, King, Judge, Light, Rock, Redeemer, Shepherd, Creator, giver of life, forgiver of sin, and one who spoke with divine authority. It's fascinating to note that in the New

Testament each and every one of those is also applied to Jesus.

The evidence for the deity of Christ is overwhelming. But there's one more attribute of God that really hits home for me because of how much I need it:

- God is also omnibenevolent (all loving).

And Jesus said in John 15:13, "Greater love has no one than this: to lay down one's life for one's friends"—*and then he did it.*

> "If you really know me, you will
> know my Father as well."
>
> JESUS, IN JOHN 14:7

35

Jesus did many things, but what was his real mission?

Jesus—who was God incarnate—came for a very specific reason. He explained in Mark 10:45, "For even the Son of Man did not come to be served, but to serve, and *to give his life as a ransom for many*" (emphasis mine).

Why would Jesus talk in terms of making a payment to release captives? The answer is *we're all captives to sin.* And because of our sin we've incurred a debt we can't afford to pay. Romans 6:23 explains, "The wages of sin is death." This means we deserve a spiritual death penalty—one we'll have to pay for all eternity.

Thankfully, Jesus came to die on the cross to pay our ransom and set us free. He "suffered once for sins, the righteous for the unrighteous,

to bring you to God" (1 Peter 3:18). This means Jesus paid the death penalty in our place. That's why Romans 6:23 ends with "but the gift of God is eternal life in Christ Jesus our Lord." No wonder the gospel is called *good news*!

But some people ask why God couldn't simply forgive people without sacrificing his Son. In response, philosopher Paul Copan, in our interview for *The Case for the Real Jesus*, points to the parable in Matthew 18:21–35, which describes a king who forgives a great debt.

"Notice what happens in that parable. The king doesn't just forgive," Copan explains. "He also absorbs the debt. The king basically says he's going to bear the burden of the loss even though the servant owes him money. Similarly, Jesus paid the cost of our sin on the cross. It's like a child who breaks a neighbor's window. He may be too young to pay the price himself, so his parents pay it for him."[8]

We're like the servant—or the child. Thankfully God, in Christ, assumed and absorbed our debt.

He paid our ransom in order to set captives like us—you and me—free for eternity.

> Here is a trustworthy saying that deserves full acceptance: Christ Jesus came into the world to save sinners—of whom I am the worst.
>
> 1 Timothy 1:15

36

The New Testament says
Jesus sweat drops of blood
when he was praying in the
Garden of Gethsemane. Is
that just a figure of speech?

That's what I thought when I was a skeptic.
Then I started my research for *The Case
for Christ*. I went to California to interview Dr.
Alexander Metherell, a physician, research scientist, and expert on the crucifixion of Jesus.

"This is a known medical condition called
hematidrosis. It's not very common, but it is associated with a high degree of psychological stress,"
he told me.

"What happens is that severe anxiety causes
the release of chemicals that break down the capillaries in the sweat glands. As a result, there's a

small amount of bleeding into these glands, and the sweat comes out tinged with blood. We're not talking about a lot of blood; it's just a very, very small amount."[9]

Interestingly, it was Luke, a physician, who noted this phenomenon. He said of Jesus in Luke 22:44: "And being in anguish, he prayed more earnestly, and his sweat was like drops of blood falling to the ground."

Jesus' anguish and passionate prayers over his impending torture and death could certainly have been enough to trigger this medical phenomenon. The *Journal of Medicine* analyzed seventy-six cases of hematidrosis and concluded that the most common causes were acute fear and intense mental contemplation.[10]

I asked Dr. Metherell what affect this bloody sweat would have had on Jesus. "What this did," he replied, "was set up the skin to be extremely fragile so that when Jesus was flogged by the Roman soldier the next day, his skin would have been very, very sensitive."

What could have prompted Jesus to willingly

endure the misery of Gethsemane, the brutality of the flogging, and the unspeakable torment of the cross?

"Well," said Dr. Metherell, "I suppose the answer can be summed up in one word—and that would be *love*."[11]

> But God demonstrates his own
> love for us in this: While we were
> still sinners, Christ died for us.

> ROMANS 5:8

37

I've heard that other faiths deny it was really Jesus who was up on the cross. How do you respond?

It's true that many Muslims deny Jesus died on the cross. What's their rationale? It's based on a single passage in the Qur'an, Surah 4:156–157, which says, "They did not kill him, nor crucified him, but so it was made to appear to them." They typically interpret this to mean that God made someone else look like Jesus, and he let that man suffer on the cross instead of him.

There are several problems with this perspective. First, why would God deceive Jesus' family and followers, and ultimately the entire world, by making us think Jesus was crucified if he really wasn't—and why would he make someone else needlessly suffer?

Second, the Qur'an does not present an eye-witness account of what happened to Jesus. It was written six hundred years after the time of Christ, and some six hundred miles from where Jesus lived, died, and was raised from the dead. Further, it doesn't even claim to be based on the accounts of anyone who saw or recorded any of those events. Rather, it claims to be based on the words of an angel who purportedly spoke to Muhammad in a cave.

Third, it contradicts the actual historical record of Jesus in the New Testament, written by his followers who walked and talked with him for three years—and who saw him die an excruciating death on the cross and then come back again three days later, fully alive.

And finally, this claim flies in the face of the actual words of Jesus—whom Muslims believe to be a prophet from God—when he predicted he was "going to be delivered into the hands of men. They will kill him, and after three days he will rise." (Mark 9:31).

We can rest assured that it really was Jesus on the cross, suffering for our sins just as he predicted, paying for our salvation just as he promised.

> "The Son of Man did not come to
> be served, but to serve, and to give
> his life as a ransom for many."

JESUS, IN MARK 10:45

38

A central claim of Christianity
is that Jesus rose from the
dead. Is there any solid
evidence to support this?

The resurrection of Christ has been called the linchpin of the Christian faith. If Jesus really did rise from the dead, then this provides power-ful evidence that his claims are true—including him being the Son of God, the prophesied Messiah, and the Savior of the World.

But if Jesus did not rise from the dead then, as the apostle Paul put it so bluntly, "your faith is futile; you are still in your sins" (1 Cor. 15:17). In other words, *this is a really big deal*!

I reasoned as a skeptic that if I could refute the resurrection claims, I'd be off the hook with the God idea altogether. So I launched what turned out to be an almost two-year investigation of the historical

evidence. What I discovered surprised me! There is a *wealth* of solid historical evidence that Jesus rose from the dead. Here's an overview, summed up in six words that start with the letter *E*:

Execution

Perhaps, I thought, Jesus just passed out on the cross or faked his death. These were once popular theories among skeptics, but they've now been thoroughly discredited. In fact, even the atheist historian Gerd Lüdemann has acknowledged that the historical evidence for Jesus' execution is "indisputable."[11]

Empty Tomb

The New Testament reports that on the first Easter morning, the women found no body in the tomb. Peter and John later confirmed this for themselves. But to me the strongest evidence is that even the enemies of Jesus implicitly admitted that the tomb was empty. Rather than refute the claims that Jesus' burial place was vacant, they made up

stories to explain *why* the body was missing (Matt. 28:11–15)—in effect, conceding that the tomb was unoccupied!

Eyewitnesses

Soon the disciples saw the risen Savior himself—some of them multiple times. Over forty days Jesus appeared to individuals and groups in a variety of circumstances. In all, we have nine ancient sources, inside and outside the New Testament, confirming the conviction of the disciples that they had encountered the risen Christ.[12]

Early Accounts

Multiple reports of Jesus' resurrection were circulating during the lifetimes of Jesus' contemporaries—people who would have been all too happy to point out the errors if the accounts had been invented. In fact, the earliest report of Jesus rising from the dead comes within *months* of his resurrection (recorded in 1 Corinthians 15:3–7)—far too quickly to have been a mere legend.

Extra-biblical Reports

Secular accounts confirm the contours of the New Testament. Historian Gary Habermas lists thirty-nine ancient sources *outside* the Bible that provide more than one hundred facts about Jesus' life, teachings, death, and resurrection.[13]

Emergence of the Church

Apart from the resurrection, it's hard to explain the beginnings of the church. Why? Because it emerged in the very city where Jesus had been crucified just a few weeks earlier—and it grew out of the claim that he had come back to life. If that claim were false, people would have laughed at the disciples. Instead, three thousand of them trusted in Christ and were baptized into the church (Acts 2:41).

I'll provide more details in the coming pages, but in the meantime I hope you can see why the case for the resurrection changed my mind—and eventually my heart and entire life.

If Christ has not been raised, your faith is futile; you are still in your sins. Then those also who have fallen asleep in Christ are lost. If only for this life we have hope in Christ, we are of all people most to be pitied. But Christ has indeed been raised from the dead, the firstfruits of those who have fallen asleep.

1 Corinthians 15:17–20

39

One gospel says Mary Magdalene and another Mary discovered Jesus' empty tomb; another gospel says only Mary did. What are we to make of discrepancies like this?

Some might call this a contradiction. What I see are differing details being emphasized by the different gospel writers. It would have been a contradiction if one gospel reported that "Mary Magdalene and the other Mary" went to the empty tomb (Matt. 28:1), and then another gospel said "*only* Mary Magdalene went to the empty tomb" (which none did).

Looking deeper, John mentions only Mary Magdalene being at the tomb (John 20:1). But if we read carefully, in the very next verse Mary tells Peter, "They have taken the Lord out of the

tomb, and we don't know where they have put him!" (v. 2). The "we" supports the other gospels when they say that other women went with Mary. John only mentions one woman by name, but uses the plural pronoun to indicate that others were with her. So there's really no conflict.

Another popular "contradiction" cited by critics involves how many angels were at Jesus' empty tomb. Some accounts mention one angel (Matt. 28:5), while others say two (John 20:12). However, it's only a contradiction if one account says that *only* one angel was at the tomb (which none do), while another account says there were two angels.

I learned as a journalist that these kinds of differences are to be expected with eyewitness accounts. Here's a modern example. The Chicago Bears play their archrival, the Green Bay Packers, twice a year during the regular football season. But do you think the Chicago newspapers file the same story, report the same events in the same order, and describe big plays in the same way as the Green Bay paper? Of course not. They watch

the same game, but emphasize the parts they deem important to their readers.

So whether in football games or biblical events, the fact that different writers highlight different details does not take away the credibility of the reports—in fact, that's to be expected.

> The angel said to the women, "Do not be afraid, for I know that you are looking for Jesus, who was crucified. He is not here; he has risen, just as he said."

MATTHEW 28:5–6

40

Some people claim Jesus' tomb was empty because someone stole his body. How do we know that's not what happened?

That same claim was made two thousand years ago. Matthew 28:12–13 reports that when Jesus' enemies heard his tomb was empty they immediately "devised a plan." Specifically,

> They gave the soldiers a large sum of money, telling them, "You are to say, 'His disciples came during the night and stole him away while we were asleep.'"

Would you like to guess how many people this scheme fooled? Approximately *zero*! Why? Because it didn't even make sense. If the guards were sleeping, they wouldn't have *known* what

happened to the body! And if they were awake, they certainly would not have let anybody steal it.

Furthermore, who would have had a motive to steal Jesus' body? Not the Jewish leaders; they wanted him dead in the first place. And certainly not the Romans; they wanted him to *stay* dead!

So that leaves us with only one other possible party: the disciples. But did they have the motive, the opportunity, or the wherewithal to take Jesus' body? Not at all! They were cowering in abject fear and regret over the death of their leader. All they wanted was to stay hidden in the shadows and out of trouble.

So to imagine that these dejected souls some-how concocted a plan to steal the body of the one who taught them never to steal, and then to tell lies about the one who taught them never to lie, all so they could be persecuted for the rest of their days while feigning a false hope over the return of their murdered Messiah . . . well, that stretches my mind beyond credulity.

For me—and I trust for you too—it's much

easier to just accept the answer that the evidence supports: the tomb was empty because Jesus had risen.

> As they entered the tomb, they saw a
> young man dressed in a white robe sitting
> on the right side, and they were alarmed.
> "Don't be alarmed," he said. "You are
> looking for Jesus the Nazarene, who was
> crucified. He has risen! He is not here."
>
> MARK 16:5–6

41

Jesus appeared to his followers after his crucifixion— but how do we know they weren't just hallucinating?

That's a question I asked when I was first investigating the resurrection. People see all kinds of strange things—Jesus on burnt toast, the Virgin Mary's tears on paintings and statues, angels peering from the clouds. Why get worked up about a handful of zealots claiming to see a risen Jesus?

Then I actually studied the matter, and found out there are good reasons to reject the hallucination hypothesis. Here are a few:

"The disciples were fearful, doubtful, and in despair after the crucifixion, whereas people who hallucinate need a fertile mind of expectancy or anticipation," Dr. Gary Habermas said to me.

"Peter was hardheaded, for goodness' sake; James was a skeptic—certainly not good candidates for hallucinations.

"Also, Habermas continued, hallucinations are comparably rare. They're usually caused by drugs or bodily deprivation. Yet we're supposed to believe that over a course of many weeks, people from all sorts of backgrounds, all kinds of temperaments, in various places, all experienced hallucinations?"[14]

In addition, psychologist Dr. Gary Collins explains, "Hallucinations are *individual* occurrences. By their very nature only one person can see a given hallucination at a time. They certainly aren't something which can be seen by a group of people."[15]

That made sense to me. If I asked you, "How did you like that dream I had last night?" you'd think I needed a bit more rest—or an appointment with Dr. Collins! Dreams, like hallucinations, are not shared events. Yet the earliest report we have about the resurrection says Jesus appeared to five hundred people at once! Besides, the disciples claimed

they talked to and even ate with the risen Jesus (1 Corinthians 15:3–7, which will be discussed further in the next answer, and Luke 24:36–48).

When you look at all of the information, it becomes clear that the disciples and others actually encountered the resurrected Jesus.

> "Why are you troubled, and why do doubts rise in your minds? Look at my hands and my feet. It is I myself! Touch me and see; a ghost does not have flesh and bones, as you see I have."

JESUS, IN LUKE 24:38–39

42

Weren't the reports of Jesus'
death and resurrection written
generations later—possibly
distorting the story?

That used to be a popular claim. But as we
touched on in answers 14 and 15, we now
know the entire New Testament, including the
four gospels, was written within the time frame
of the lives of Jesus' contemporaries—not generations later.[16] So there was simply not enough time
for legend to replace the historical facts that were
relayed by those early reporters.

But here's what's interesting: as early as the
Gospels were, they were preceded by the even
earlier writings of the apostle Paul. In one letter
that Paul wrote within twenty-five years after the
death of Christ, he includes a creed that had been
formulated previously by the earliest Christians
and then handed down to him:

For what I received I passed on to you as of first importance: that Christ died for our sins according to the Scriptures, that he was buried, that he was raised on the third day according to the Scriptures, and that he appeared to Cephas, and then to the Twelve. After that, he appeared to more than five hundred of the brothers and sisters at the same time, most of whom are still living, though some have fallen asleep. Then he appeared to James, then to all the apostles. (1 Cor. 15:3–7)

"Many scholars believe Paul received this creed from Peter and James while visiting with them in Jerusalem three years after his conversion," said New Testament scholar Michael Licona. "That would be within five years of the crucifixion. Think about that—it's really amazing! Not only is it extremely early, but it was apparently given to Paul by eyewitnesses or others he deemed reliable, which heightens its credibility even more."[17]

Since the beliefs that make up that early creed go back even further in time, this means we have

a report of the resurrection that goes back virtually to the cross itself. Said historian James D. G. Dunn: "This tradition, we can be entirely confident, was formulated as tradition within months of Jesus' death."[18]

Put another way, *we have a news flash from the ancient world*!

> For we did not follow cleverly devised
> stories when we told you about the coming
> of our Lord Jesus Christ in power, but
> we were eyewitnesses of his majesty.
>
> 2 PETER 1:16

43

What difference does it make today that a man rose from the dead two thousand years ago?

I once wondered the same thing—but soon realized the implications of Jesus' resurrection were huge. Here are three examples:

The resurrection establishes Jesus' identity.

After being asked by the Pharisees for some kind of proof that he was who he claimed to be, Jesus said in Matthew 12:39–40, "A wicked and adulterous generation asks for a sign! But none will be given it except the sign of the prophet Jonah. For as Jonah was three days and three nights in the belly of a huge fish, so the Son of Man will be three days and three nights in the heart of the earth." Jesus made it clear that the ultimate validation

of his claims would be his own death, burial, and resurrection. These would show that he truly was the Son of God.

The resurrection validates the Christian faith.

This point flows from the last one. As the unique Son of God, Jesus is "calling God his own Father, making himself equal with God" (John 5:18). This validates the Christian doctrine of the Trinity— one God in three persons—Father, Son, and Holy Spirit. And because Jesus is God, he is also Lord, so we need to believe and obey him (Luke 6:46; Matt. 28:20).

The resurrection energizes the gospel message.

Jesus came "to give his life as a ransom for many" (Matt. 20:28). Paul explains this further: "He was delivered over to death for our sins and was raised to life for our justification" (Rom. 4:25). Both elements are key to the gospel: Jesus' *death* made the necessary payment; Jesus' *resurrection* enabled him to apply that payment and to give us

life. He has provided everything. All we need to do is say yes, and to follow him as our forgiver and leader.

> But Christ has indeed been raised from the dead, the firstfruits of those who have fallen asleep. For since death came through a man, the resurrection of the dead comes also through a man. For as in Adam all die, so in Christ all will be made alive.
>
> 1 Corinthians 15:20–22

44

How can belief in the resurrection of Christ impact someone personally?

I posed that question to Dr. Gary Habermas, one of the world's leading resurrection scholars. His answer harkened back to an earlier time in his life, when his wife, Debbie, was slowly dying of stomach cancer. Caught off guard by the tenderness of the moment, all I could do was listen.

"I sat on our porch," he began. "My wife was upstairs dying. Except for a few weeks, she was home through it all. It was the worst thing that could possibly happen.

"But do you know what was amazing? My students would call me and say, 'At a time like this, aren't you glad about the resurrection?' As sober as those circumstances were, I had to smile for two reasons. First, my students were trying to

cheer me up with my own teaching. And second, it worked.

"I knew if God were to come to me, I'd ask only one question: 'Lord, why is Debbie up there in bed?' And I think God would respond by asking gently, 'Gary, did I raise my Son from the dead?'

"I'd say, 'Come on, Lord, I've written seven books on that topic! Of course he was raised from the dead. But I want to know about Debbie!'

"I think he'd keep coming back to the same question—'Did I raise my Son from the dead?' 'Did I raise my Son from the dead?'—until I got his point: the resurrection says that if Jesus was raised two thousand years ago, there's an answer to Debbie's death in 1995. And do you know what? It worked for me while I was sitting on the porch, and it still works today."

Habermas locked eyes with mine. "That's not some sermon," he said quietly. "I believe that with all my heart. If there's a resurrection, there's a heaven. If Jesus was raised, Debbie was raised. And I will be someday too.

"Then I'll see them both."[19]

And if the Spirit of him who raised
Jesus from the dead is living in you, he
who raised Christ from the dead will
also give life to your mortal bodies
because of his Spirit who lives in you.

Romans 8:11

45

Isn't it narrow-minded to claim that Jesus is the only pathway to God?

It certainly would be narrow-minded if Christians were saying, "Jesus is the only way because he's *my* way," or if they were just trying to edge out the competition from other religions. But this idea did not originate with some pastor or theologian. It goes back to Jesus himself. He's the one who said, "I am the way and the truth and the life. No one comes to the Father except through me" (John 14:6).

People who bristle at this idea are ultimately arguing with Jesus—not with the Christians who are simply trying to be faithful to his teachings.

But was *Jesus* narrow-minded? Well, in a sense he was. In fact, in the Sermon on the Mount

he said, "Enter through the narrow gate. For wide is the gate and broad is the road that leads to destruction, and many enter through it. But small is the gate and narrow the road that leads to life, and only a few find it" (Matt. 7:13–14).

If Jesus was right about this, then he was being appropriately narrow-minded. He was being like parents who are narrow enough to insist that their children walk on the sidewalk and not in the street, or a doctor who limits his prescriptions to medicine that will actually help people rather than poison them, or the airline pilot who restricts his landing options to that narrow path to life called a runway, rather than trying to put the airplane down on a cornfield or a beach.

You see, we really *want* narrow approaches— as long as they are based on truth and point us in the direction that's best for us.

Jesus gave us every reason to believe he was telling the truth, and that he loves us enough to lead us toward forgiveness, life, and an eternity with him.

"I am the gate; whoever enters through
me will be saved. They will come
in and go out, and find pasture. The
thief comes only to steal and kill and
destroy; I have come that they may
have life, and have it to the full."

JESUS, IN JOHN 10:9–10

Answers to Other Challenges to Christianity

46

There are so many other religions out there. How can we be sure that Christianity is the right one?

No doubt about it—people believe all kinds of religious ideas, and most people are

sincere in their beliefs. We should treat them with gentleness and respect (1 Peter 3:15), and do all we can to protect their rights—as well as our own—to practice religion freely.

I also know that *people can be sincere, but sincerely wrong*. In fact it's impossible that all the religions could be right, since they contradict each other on so many fundamental points. For example, look at what these religions teach about God:

- Buddhism historically denies that God exists (*atheism*).
- Hinduism teaches that everything is part of an all-pervasive, impersonal god (*pantheism*).
- Christianity teaches that there is one God who is personal and who created everything (*theism*).

As one person put it, if all these religions are true, then God must be schizophrenic—because he doesn't even know who he is, but tells one

group one thing about himself while telling others something completely different!

Well, God is not schizophrenic—so we're forced to choose between belief systems. How should we do this? Should we base our decision on our traditions, or on what some authority figure tells us to believe, or perhaps on what we feel in our hearts? Those are dangerous ways to decide.

My contention, and the approach I've used throughout my writings, is that we should choose our beliefs based on where logic and the evidence point (while asking God for guidance). And it's with that approach that I've concluded Christianity—over any other worldview—squares with the facts of science, philosophy, and history.

More than that, my own experience has borne this out. Psalm 34:8 invites us, "Taste and see that the Lord is good; blessed is the one who takes refuge in him." Well, as one who has been tasting and seeing for more than three decades—and experiencing those blessings—I can testify that the psalmist was right: the Lord is real, and he is good.

"I am the LORD your God,
who teaches you what is best for you,
who directs you in the way you should go."

ISAIAH 48:17

47

Isn't it elitist to say that people must be followers of Jesus in order to get into heaven?

It can certainly sound that way—and unfortunately some Christians project an air of arrogance and exclusivity in how they live out their faith and then communicate it to others. But authentic Christianity is anything but arrogant or exclusive. Let me illustrate.

Imagine two country clubs. The first has a strict set of rules and only allows people in who have earned their membership. They have to accomplish something, obtain superior wisdom, or fulfill a long list of demands and requirements in order to qualify for acceptance. And despite their best efforts, lots of people just won't make the grade and will therefore be excluded.

In effect, this is what other religious systems are like.

The second country club throws its doors wide open and says, "Anybody who wants membership is invited inside. Rich or poor, black or white, regardless of your ethnic heritage or where you live, we would love to include you. Entry will be based not on your qualifications or efforts but only on accepting this invitation. So we'll leave the matter up to you. The offer stands. You decide. But we will never turn you away if you sincerely and humbly seek admittance."

That's what Christianity is like.

Which country club is being snobbish? Christians aren't being exclusive; they're being inclusive. They're not being haughty; they're being hospitable. They're not pretending to be better or more accomplished than anyone else. Instead, they admit their own weakness and invite others who feel weak or needy to join them in order to find the help that they've found through Christ.

Preacher D. T. Niles summed up genuine Christianity well when he explained that we are simply "one beggar telling another beggar where to find food."[1]

The Spirit and the bride say, "Come!"
And let the one who hears say,
"Come!" Let the one who is thirsty
come; and let the one who wishes take
the free gift of the water of life.

REVELATION 22:17

48

Why does God allow tragedy and suffering?

You see it all over the news: wildfires, floods, hurricanes, tornadoes, and earthquakes—as well as senseless shootings, acts of terror, and wars. In addition, there is the everyday pain in individual lives: illness, abuse, broken relationships, betrayal, sorrow, injuries, heartache, crime, and death.

People are suffering all around us. And many ask, "Why? Why did God allow this?"

Jesus predicted these things would happen. Unlike some religious leaders who wrote off evil and suffering as mere illusions, Jesus dealt with reality. He said in John 16:33, "You will have suffering in this world" (HCSB).

But, again, why? I cannot stand in the shoes of God and give a complete answer, but we can understand some things.

To illustrate, Leslie and I were driving from Chicago to Door County, Wisconsin. It was dark when it started raining heavily, and then we hit dense fog. I could barely see the line on the edge of the highway and didn't know what to do. Then a truck went by us, traveling at a confident and deliberate pace. We could see his taillights through the fog, and realized that if we could just follow those lights, we'd be headed in the right direction.

It is similar with tragedy and suffering. We may not be able to make out all the peripheral details of why, but there are some biblical truths that can illuminate some helpful points of light for us. And if we'll follow those lights, they will lead us toward conclusions I believe can satisfy our hearts and souls. Let me mention five that I've found helpful.

First Point of Light: God is not the creator of evil and suffering.

Genesis 1:31 says everything God made "was very good." But if God is not the author of evil, then where did it come from? God created us with free will so we could love him—because real love always entails

the ability to love or not to love. Unfortunately, we abused our freedom by rejecting God's love and walking away from him. And that resulted in the introduction of evil into our lives and into the world.

Second Point of Light: Though suffering is not good, God can use it to accomplish good.

Romans 8:28 promises: "In all things God works for the good of those who love him, who have been called according to his purpose." Notice it doesn't say that God causes the evil and suffering, just that he will cause some kind of good to emerge. And it doesn't say we will see immediately or even in this life how God has brought good out of the bad circumstance—just that it will happen for those of us who love him.

Third Point of Light: The day is coming when suffering will cease and God will judge evil.

"If God has the power to vanquish evil and suffering," people ask, "then why doesn't he do it?" But

just because he hasn't done it yet doesn't mean he won't do it. The Bible says the day will come when sickness and pain will be eradicated and people will be held accountable for the evil they've committed. Justice will be served (Rev. 20:12; 21:4).

Also, "the Lord is not slow in keeping his promise . . . He is patient with you, not wanting anyone to perish, but everyone to come to repentance" (2 Peter 3:9). In other words, God hasn't vanquished evil yet because he's waiting to first reach some of us!

Fourth Point of Light: Our suffering will pale in comparison to what God has in store for his followers.

Paul said in Romans 8:18: "I consider that our present sufferings are not worth comparing with the glory that will be revealed in us." This is not to deny the reality of pain in our lives. But after 354,484,545 days of pure bliss in heaven, we'll look back and realize that these difficult days aren't worth comparing to an eternity of blessings and joy with him.

Fifth Point of Light: We decide whether to turn bitter or turn to God for peace and courage.

We've all seen examples of how the same suffering that causes one person to turn bitter and reject God can cause another person to turn to God. We all make the choice to either run away from God or run to him. But as one who's tried both responses, let me assure you it's much better to run *to* him!

Let me finish the story of Leslie and me in Wisconsin. We were following the taillights of that truck when the fog slowly began to lift, the rain let up, and we entered a town with some lights. And there, silhouetted against the night sky, we saw the steeple of a church and the cross of Christ. After driving through the confusion of the fog for so long, that image struck me with poignancy I'll never forget—because it was through the cross that Jesus conquered the world for us.

God's ultimate answer to suffering isn't an

explanation; it's his incarnation. He isn't some distant, detached, and disinterested deity; he entered our world and personally experienced our pain.

Jesus is there in the lowest places of our lives. As philosopher Peter Kreeft says, "Are we broken? He was broken, like bread, for us. Are we despised? He was despised and rejected of men. Do we cry out that we can't take anymore? He was a man of sorrows and acquainted with grief. Did someone betray us? He was sold out. Are our most tender relationships broken? He too loved and was rejected."[2]

Jesus is much closer than your closest friend. Because if you've put your trust in him, then he is *in* you. And, therefore, your sufferings are his sufferings; your sorrow is his sorrow.

So when tragedy strikes, when suffering comes, when you're wrestling with pain—and when you make the choice to run into his arms, here's what you're going to discover: peace to deal with the present, courage to deal with your future, and the incredible promise of eternal life in heaven.

"I have told you these things so that in Me you may have peace. You will have suffering in this world. But be courageous! I have conquered the world."

JESUS, IN JOHN 16:33 HCSB

49

Can God really bring good out of evil?

If God truly is all-wise, then he knows not only the present but also the future. And if God truly is love, then he could allow awful things to happen because he foresees that in the long run more people will be better off than if he had miraculously intervened and prevented those things from happening.

God has shown how this can work in the Old Testament. Joseph was tricked by his jealous brothers, sold into slavery, falsely accused, and ended up alone and forgotten in prison. These things certainly were evil, and God could have intervened along the way. Instead, he brought good out of these things by using them to bring Joseph to a place of leadership under the Pharaoh, through which he was able to protect, feed, and

ultimately save Joseph's family during a severe famine (Gen. 37–50).

Joseph later explained to his brothers: "You intended to harm me, but God intended it for good to accomplish what is now being done, the saving of many lives" (Gen. 50:20).

God did this in a much greater way by taking the very *worst* thing that has ever happened and turning it into the very *best* thing that has ever happened—the death of Jesus on the cross. At the time, nobody could see how anything good could come from such a horrific event. But God knew the result would be the opening of heaven to all people who follow him. So the most horrible tragedy in all of history was later seen as the most glorious event of all time.

If it can happen there—if the ultimate evil resulted in the ultimate good—then it can happen elsewhere, including in our own lives.

So remember, as you face trials and suffering, when you can't imagine anything positive emerging, you can trust in the God who brings good

from bad. He did it for Joseph, he did it for Jesus, and he can do it for you.

> And we know that in all things God works
> for the good of those who love him, who
> have been called according to his purpose.

ROMANS 8:28

50

How does our sense of morality point to God's existence?

"On what basis is something considered good or evil, right or wrong?" asks my colleague Mark Mittelberg in *The Questions Christians Hope No One Will Ask*. "And where did this basis come from? Did it start with the Big Bang? I can just imagine it: billions of years ago . . . a massive explosion . . . galaxies emerging from the fiery blast. And then, out of the gaseous flames, 'Thou shalt act altruistically; thou shalt be kind to the underprivileged; thou shalt love thine enemies; thou shalt not steal; and—oh yes—thou shalt maintain a moderately small carbon footprint' (all in perfect King James English, of course).

"No one really believes that moral values emerge out of physical explosions. So where did they come from? Atheists are hard-pressed to

provide an answer for the existence of *objective* moral values."[3]

Dr. William Lane Craig elaborates: "Objective moral values are valid and binding independently of whether anyone believes in them or not. For example, to label the Holocaust objectively wrong is to say it was wrong even though the Nazis thought it was right. Now, if God does not exist, then moral values are not objective in this way."[4]

"We know that murder and rape and bigotry and racism are wrong—really, objectively wrong—regardless of traditions, customs, or preferences," Mittelberg continues. "But where did we get this knowledge—this intrinsic sense of right and wrong? If we didn't invent it, if it transcends the realms of culture and politics, if it's something we can't get away from, then what is its source? Could it be that a Moral Lawgiver actually knit those moral standards, along with the ability to understand and operate by them, into the very fabric of what it means to be human?"[5]

I think that's exactly what it means, and it's a

powerful reminder that there is a good God—one worth following wholeheartedly.

> The requirements of the law are written
> on their hearts, their consciences also
> bearing witness, and their thoughts
> sometimes accusing them and at
> other times even defending them.
>
> ROMANS 2:15

51

How could a loving God
send people to hell?

When I hear this question I immediately
want to set the record straight: *God does
not send anyone to hell!* He makes it clear that he
wants everyone to come to him for forgiveness
and eternal life. First Timothy 2:4–6 tells us God
"wants all people to be saved and to come to a
knowledge of the truth." It adds that God provided
Jesus to be the mediator between us and him, and
assures us that he "gave himself as a ransom for
all people."

Based on passages like this, we can be confident God does not want anyone in hell—and made
provision for everyone to escape it. But Jesus also
said, "Wide is the gate and broad is the road that
leads to destruction, and many enter through it"

(Matt. 7:13). So if God doesn't want people to end up there, why is it so many apparently do?

I talked to philosopher J. P. Moreland about this. "He has made us with free will," the philosopher explained. "And he has made us for a purpose: to relate lovingly to him and to others. If we fail over and over again to live for the purpose for which we were made . . . then God will have absolutely no choice but to give us what we've asked for all along in our lives, which is separation from him.

"Hell was not part of the original creation. Hell is God's fall-back position. Hell is something God was forced to make because people chose to rebel against him and turn against what was best for them and the purpose for which they were created."

I asked Moreland how people should respond to these truths.

"For those who don't know Christ, it should motivate them to redouble their efforts to seek him and to find him," he replied. "For those of us

who know him, it should cause us to redouble our efforts to extend his message of mercy and grace to those who need it."[6]

I would simply add a double Amen.

> The Lord is not slow in keeping his
> promise . . . Instead he is patient with
> you, not wanting anyone to perish,
> but everyone to come to repentance.
>
> 2 Peter 3:9

52

What about people who have never heard about Jesus or the gospel—how will God deal with them?

This is one of the most commonly asked questions about Christianity—and frankly, it's challenging because we don't have the complete answer. God hasn't explicitly told us how he is going to deal with these situations. But we do know a few things about the matter.

First, we know from the Bible that everyone has a moral standard written on their hearts by God, and that everybody is guilty of violating that standard. That's why our conscience bothers us when we do something wrong.

Second, we know that everyone has enough information from observing the created world to know that God exists, but people have suppressed

it and rejected God anyway—for which they rightfully deserve punishment (Rom. 1:18–20).

Third, we know from both the Old and New Testaments that those who seek God will find him. Jesus said, for example, in Matthew 7:7, "Ask and it will be given to you; seek and you will find; knock and the door will be opened to you." The Bible also indicates that the Holy Spirit is seeking us first, making it possible for us to in turn seek him (John 16:7–11). This suggests to me that people who respond to the understanding that they have and who earnestly seek after the one true God will find an opportunity, in some way, to receive the eternal life that he has graciously provided through Jesus Christ.

Fourth, we see repeatedly in Scripture that God is scrupulously fair. Genesis 18:25 asks, "Will not the Judge of all the earth do right?" Said author Ronald Nash: "When God is finished dealing with all of us, none will be able to complain that they were treated unfairly."[7]

Finally, we know that apart from the payment

Christ made on the cross, nobody has a chance to getting off of death row. But exactly how much knowledge a person must have about Jesus or precisely where the lines of faith are drawn, only God knows. He and he alone can expose the motives of a person's heart.

Let me add that, without exception, every time I've heard this question it has been from someone who *has* heard about Jesus. As important as this theoretical discussion is regarding the fate of those who have never heard, I need to remind thaose people that they have heard the good news and that they are responsible for what they do with it. In fact, Jesus said in Luke 12:48, "From everyone who has been given much, much will be demanded; and from the one who has been entrusted with much, much more will be asked."

My strong encouragement to you, or to the friend who asked you this question, is to respond to God's gracious offer of salvation through Christ and then join those of us who are doing all we can to spread his love and truth to everyone we can

possibly reach—especially those who have never heard the good news.

> "For everyone who asks receives; the one who seeks finds; and to the one who knocks, the door will be opened."

JESUS, IN MATTHEW 7:8

53

I found out the word *Trinity* isn't in the Bible. Why does the church teach it?

It is true that the word *Trinity* is not in the Bible—but neither are the words *theology, incarnation,* or *omniscience.* The Bible teaches many concepts without using their modern labels. But the doctrine of the Trinity is clearly taught in Scripture.

Here are four truths the Bible makes clear.[8]

There is only one true God.

Deuteronomy 6:4 declares, "Hear, O Israel: The LORD our God, the LORD is one." This is the *Shema,* the central teaching of Judaism. And the apostle Paul confirms in the New Testament that "there is but one God" (1 Cor. 8:6).

The Father is God.

It is clear that the Father is God in 2 Peter 1:17: "[Jesus] received honor and glory from God the Father when the voice came to him from the Majestic Glory, saying, 'This is my Son, whom I love; with him I am well pleased.'"

The Son is God.

Jesus said in John 8:58, "Before Abraham was born, I am!"—affirming his preexistence while also applying the divine "I AM" name for God from Exodus 3:14 to himself. In John 10:30, Jesus said, "I and the Father are one," with the Greek word for "one" meaning "one in essence or nature." In both instances, his theologically astute listeners understood his divine claim—and tried to stone him for blasphemy. John 5:18 declares, "For this reason they tried all the more to kill him . . . he was even calling God his own Father, making himself equal with God."

Jesus accepted worship (Matt. 8:2), which is reserved for God alone, and forgave sins (Mark

2:5), which only God can do. He affirmed Thomas when the disciple said to him, "My Lord and my God!" (John 20:28). He is called "our great God and Savior" (Titus 2:13). Colossians 2:9 says that in him "all the fullness of the Deity lives in bodily form." He is described as the one who created all things in John 1:3 and Colossians 1:16. And the Father calls him "God" in Hebrews 1:8.

Asked by the high priest at his trial, "Are you the Messiah, the Son of the Blessed One?" Jesus replied, "I am . . . And you will see the Son of Man sitting at the right hand of the Mighty One and coming on the clouds of heaven" (Mark 14:61–62)—referring to the divine figure in Daniel 7:13–14. The high priest immediately recognized that Jesus was claiming to be God.

The Holy Spirit is God

The Holy Spirit is called God in Acts 5:3–4. He possesses the attributes of deity (1 Cor. 2:10–11), and is associated with God the Father in creation (Gen. 1:2) and with other members of the Trinity in Matthew 28:18–20.

Putting this together, the doctrine of the Trinity uniquely accounts for all four biblical truths: it shows that God is a "Tri-unity"—"Tri-" (meaning three persons; truths #2–4) in "unity" (in one God; truth #1). The common way of explaining this is *there is one God who eternally exists in three persons: Father, Son, and Holy Spirit.*

As theologian Norman Geisler pointed out, this is not a self-contradictory doctrine. "The Trinity is not the belief that God is three persons and only one person at the same time and in the same sense. That would be a contradiction," he said. "Rather, it is the belief that there are three persons in one *nature.* This may be a mystery, but it is not a contradiction."[9]

When asked why God doesn't make this more simple instead of so complicated, apologist Mark Mittelberg replies, "This isn't an idea God invented for our ease of consumption. *It is his revelation of who he actually is.* When we realize we're talking about the eternal, almighty Creator of the universe, it shouldn't surprise us that he a being whose nature is a bit difficult for our puny minds to fully grasp!"[10]

Because the Trinity reflects God's own self-revelation, it's a doctrine we should hold on to tightly—and defend strongly.

"Therefore go and make disciples of all nations, baptizing them in the name of the Father and of the Son and of the Holy Spirit, and teaching them to obey everything I have commanded you."

JESUS, IN MATTHEW 28:19–20

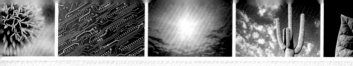

54

Why do I still struggle with doubts about my faith—and what can I do about it?

No doubt about it: doubt scares many Christians. They stare into the dark, pestered by uncertainties and questions that make them feel anxious and vulnerable. When those times come, keep this in mind:

- Doubt is not the opposite of faith; the opposite is *unbelief.*
- Doubt is normal. Virtually every thinking person—regardless of beliefs—at times has doubts.
- Even King David, John the Baptist, and the apostle Thomas doubted—yet they are considered heroes of our faith.

- Doubts are not necessarily destructive; they can actually strengthen our faith.

How should we respond to doubt?

Step #1: Find the root of your doubt.

Is it intellectual, caused by questions in your mind? Or emotional, based on things you feel (or don't feel)? Or does it stem from your will—choices you make that hamper your relationship with God?

Step #2: Ask God and others for help.

When we suppress our doubts, we unwittingly give them more power. But when we admit them to God and to mature Christian friends, it's amazing how their potency dissipates. Don't try to face them alone.

Step #3: Implement a course of treatment.

Do you wrestle with intellectual doubts? Read great books, do extra research, and talk to Christians who have grappled with the same issues. Emotional doubts? Discuss them with a pastor or Christian counselor. Doubts related to your will? Let God

guide your daily decisions—*really obey him*—and you will experience breakthroughs.

Step #4: Take scrupulous care of your spiritual health.

A healthy faith is the best antidote for the virus of doubt. Prioritize the daily habits and relationships that will keep you spiritually strong—prayer, Scripture reading, study, worship, and fellowship.

Step #5: Hold your remaining questions in tension.

Accept the fact that there are always more questions—and rejoice in knowing we'll have an eternity in heaven to get all the answers!

> "If you hold to my teaching, you are really my disciples. Then you will know the truth, and the truth will set you free."
>
> JESUS, IN JOHN 8:31–32

Postlude

Turning Answers into Action

55

Some people believe Jesus is the Son of God who died and rose again, but say, "So what?" How do you respond to them?

That's a challenging question. Apathy runs deep in our culture—and too often in the church as well. In fact, studies show that many who sit in services each week do not actually believe many things the Bible teaches and have never really put their trust in Christ.

Along with praying for God to open their eyes, we can try to help them see the implications of what they claim to believe. Here are some realizations I had at the end of my search for God:

- If Jesus is the Son of God, his words are more than just good ideas from a wise teacher; they are divine insights on which I can confidently build my life.
- If Jesus sets the standard for morality, I can now have an unwavering foundation for my choices and decisions, rather than basing them on the ever-shifting sands of expediency and self-centeredness.
- If Jesus did rise from the dead, he's still alive today and available for me to encounter on a personal basis.

- If Jesus conquered death, he can open the door of eternal life for me too.
- If Jesus has divine power, he has the supernatural ability to guide me and help me and transform me as I follow him.
- If Jesus personally knows the pain of loss and suffering, he can comfort and encourage me in the midst of the turbulence that he himself warned is inevitable in a world corrupted by sin.
- If Jesus loves me as he says, he has my best interests at heart. That means I have nothing to lose and everything to gain by committing myself to him and his purposes.
- If Jesus is who he claims to be, then as my Creator he rightfully deserves my allegiance, obedience, and worship.

In light of these great truths, how could anyone *not* want to turn and follow Christ?

Therefore, since the promise of entering his rest still stands, let us be careful that none of you be found to have fallen short of it . . . "Today, if you hear his voice, do not harden your hearts."

HEBREWS 4:1, 7

56

You've said you came to realize
you didn't have enough faith
to maintain your atheism. Can
you explain what you mean?

There's a lot of confusion about *faith*. Some
believe faith actually contradicts facts. "The
whole point of faith," scoffed Michael Shermer
of *The Skeptical Inquirer*, "is to believe regardless
of the evidence, which is the very antithesis of
science."[1]

That's not my understanding. I see faith as
*a reasonable step in the same direction that the
evidence is pointing*. It's doing what I did as a journalist—following the facts wherever they lead
and then making a sound conclusion based on the
weight of the information, even though I couldn't
prove something 100 percent.

Given that definition, it's easy to see that

every point of view, religious or secular, involves a measure of faith. As an atheist, for example, I concluded that there was no God based on what I thought to be good reasons, even though I couldn't prove he didn't exist. That was faith.

But when I started investigating Christianity, I began finding more and more evidence pointing away from atheism and toward belief in God. As I looked into science, for example, I realized I'd previously accepted, largely by faith, these misguided ideas:

- Nothing produces everything.
- Non-life produces life.
- Randomness produces finely tuned design.
- Chaos produces information.
- Unconsciousness produces consciousness.
- Non-reason produces reason.

In addition, I discovered that the historical evidence establishes the reliability of the New Testament, demonstrates the fulfillment of ancient prophecies in the life of Jesus, and supports the

reality of Jesus' resurrection—authenticating his claim to being the unique Son of God.

The range, variety, depth, and breathtaking persuasive power of the evidence, from both science and history, affirmed the credibility of Christianity to the degree that my doubts simply washed away.

In the end, putting my trust in the God of the Bible was nothing less than the most rational decision I could make. I merely permitted the torrent of facts to carry me along to their most logical conclusion: *faith in Christ makes sense like nothing else.*

Now faith is confidence in
what we hope for and assurance
about what we do not see.

HEBREWS 11:1

57

Christians say that God's
salvation and eternal life are
the most important things
we can ever have. How can
I make sure they're mine?

A lot of people think it is mostly what we *do*
that determines whether we'll receive God's
salvation. To them the equation for eternal life
looks like this:

Jesus + Good Works = Eternal Life

According to this approach, people may have
some understanding about Christ, but they think
their own efforts to be good people will largely
determine whether they end up in heaven.

Yet there's a problem: they can never feel

confident they've fulfilled this equation and actually earned eternal life. It's like someone running in a race where there's no finish line. These folks might work frantically, but they never know if they've done enough. Many simply give up. Unfortunately, Romans 3:23 makes it clear that we never can do enough. Regardless of our efforts, we all "fall short of the glory of God."

But Ephesians 2:8–9 says, "For it is by grace you have been saved." What is grace? Grace is an unearned blessing. It is a free gift. And how do we get that gift? The passage goes on to explain, "For it is by grace you have been saved, through faith—and this is not from yourselves, it is the gift of God—not by works, so that no one can boast."

So it's *not* by our efforts. Instead, we must put our trust in Jesus—the one who lived a perfect life on our behalf and then died on the cross to pay the penalty we owed. Accordingly, the biblical formula looks like this:

Jesus + Nothing = Eternal Life

What is eternal life? It is a relationship with the living God that begins the moment you trust in Christ and continues for eternity.

Some people look at this and say, "So good works are out—you're saying it doesn't matter what you do?" It's a good question. Going back to the Ephesians passage, we see this in the very next verse (v. 10): "For we are God's handiwork, created in Christ Jesus to do good works, which God prepared in advance for us to do" (v. 10).

Good works *do* play a role in the Christian life, but here's the critically important distinction: they're not a *means* of gaining eternal life; rather, they are a *result* that flows out of it. So here's what the completed equation looks like:

Jesus + Nothing = Eternal Life + Good Works

What we do as Christians really does matter— but not as a means to earn our way into heaven. Rather, we're so overwhelmed by God's mercy and compassion that we just naturally want to share his love with other people.

Do you see the difference? It's not a feverish "I've got to work my way to heaven" mentality. Rather, it's a grateful "God, you are so gracious that I just want to serve you out of a heart full of love" kind of response. What a difference—and what a relief! More than that, what an opportunity for us and our friends: All we need to do is turn from our sins and failed religious efforts and ask Jesus to be our savior—and he takes care of the rest.

But when the kindness and love of
God our Savior appeared, he saved us,
not because of righteous things we
had done, but because of his mercy.

TITUS 3:4—5

58

Why are some Christians so adamant about telling everyone else about their faith? Shouldn't we just let people come to their own conclusions?

There's no question that sometimes Christians can be overbearing. But it typically stems from good motives. It generally flows out of the urgency that comes from the realization that we never know when death will come knocking.

Often, we don't get any warning before a heart attack strikes, a drunk driver crosses the centerline, a wildfire or flood sweeps through a canyon, or an airplane loses power. So the question we're compelled to ask people is this: *"Are you ready?"*

One of the first verses I memorized as a Christian was 1 John 5:13: "I write these things to

you who believe in the name of the Son of God so that you may know that you have eternal life."

God doesn't want us to be wondering or steeped in anxiety over whether we're headed for heaven. He says we can *know*.

The Bible also makes it clear that we can be religious but not be in a right relationship with God. Religious activities and affiliations never saved anyone. Salvation comes from knowing Christ personally and receiving his provision for our sin. But it doesn't happen automatically. It doesn't come by attending a great church, being baptized, taking communion, or hanging out with a bunch of Christians. It comes from deciding to turn from your sins, to stop trusting in your own resources, and to accept the forgiveness and eternal life that Jesus purchased on the cross for you. *That* is how you gain God's peace and confidence.

At the risk of sounding overbearing, I want to tell everyone I can to settle it now, so that their eternity with God will be secure if tragedy were to strike. And if you haven't done so, or if you aren't sure that you have, I would urge you to

receive the forgiveness and leadership of Christ right away as well.

Then you can know that even if the very worst thing were to happen to you today, it will immediately be followed by the very best thing of all.

> For to me, to live is Christ
> and to die is gain.
>
> PHILIPPIANS 1:21

59

It's hard to believe that God can just snap his fingers and suddenly I'm forgiven and my sins are all wiped away. Isn't there more to it than that?

I know, it sounds too good to be true. Our problem is that we mistakenly think God's forgiveness is like human forgiveness. Thankfully, it's not.

- People are often reluctant to forgive. But Psalm 86:5 assures us, "You, LORD, are forgiving and good, abounding in love to all who call to you."
- People forgive but sometimes don't forget—and later dredge up your mistakes and throw them in your face. Isaiah 43:25 says, "I, even I, am he who blots out your transgressions,

for my own sake, and remembers your sins no more." Micah 7:19 adds, "You will ... tread our sins underfoot and hurl all our iniquities into the depths of the sea."

- **People forgive minor sins but often hold on to major hurts.** Isaiah 1:18 says, "Though your sins are like scarlet, they shall be as white as snow; though they are red as crimson, they shall be like wool."

- **People put conditions on forgiveness.** Isaiah 55:7 says, "Let the wicked forsake their ways and the unrighteous their thoughts. Let them turn to the Lord, and he will have mercy on them, and to our God, for he will freely pardon."

- **People may forgive one or two mistakes but then draw the line and say, "That's it, no more."** Lamentations 3:21–23 says, "Yet this I call to mind and therefore I have hope: Because of the Lord's great love we are not consumed, for his compassions never fail. They are new every morning; great is your faithfulness."

- People forgive but can hold a grudge. "For I will forgive their wickedness," God said in Jeremiah 31:34, "and will remember their sins no more."

Let me add that God did much more than "just snap his fingers." He purchased our salvation with the highest price that's ever been paid: the shed blood of his precious Son. So the gift was expensive, but the offer is free.

No wonder they call it *amazing* grace.

> If we confess our sins, he is faithful and
> just and will forgive us our sins and
> purify us from all unrighteousness.
>
> 1 JOHN 1:9

60

Now that we've explored a lot
of questions and answers, what
should I do with the information?

If you're already a follower of Christ, then I
trust that for you, as for me, the rigors of intellectual scrutiny have helped your faith emerge
deeper, richer, more resilient, and more certain
than ever. I hope this culminates in your having
a truly confident faith—and that it emboldens you
to share that faith with others.

If you're not yet a Christian, I trust that by
reading answer after answer in this book you're
discovering, as I did, that the case for Christianity
is powerful and persuasive. If so, all that's left
now is to talk to God and tell him you're ready to
turn from your sins and receive his grace through
Christ. Then you'll become his son or daughter,

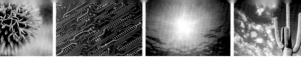

embarking on a spiritual adventure that will last throughout your lifetime—and into eternity.

But maybe important questions still linger. Perhaps I didn't address the objection that's uppermost in your mind. If so, I hope the information in these pages will at least encourage you to continue your investigation. I'd also like to echo the advice I gave at the beginning of the book:

1. Keep pursuing your search as a front-burner issue.

C. S. Lewis said that "Christianity is . . . if true, of infinite importance."[2] Knowing that, keep seeking answers diligently.

2. Keep your mind open and continue to follow the evidence.

I hope some of my other *Case* books will help with that process, as well as what's been written by the many experts I've quoted throughout these answers. And be sure to study the Bible as well. For further information see the Recommended Resources page in the back of this book.

3. When the evidence is in, reach a verdict.

Resolve that once you've gathered a sufficient amount of information, you'll make a decision, knowing you'll never have full resolution of every single issue. You may even want to whisper a prayer in the meantime, asking God to guide you to the truth about him.

And through it all, you'll have my sincere encouragement as you continue taking steps toward Christ.

> "You will seek me and find me when
> you seek me with all your heart."
>
> JEREMIAH 29:13

Notes

I. Prelude: Seeking Spiritual Answers

1. Blaise Pascal, *Pensees* (Stilwell, KS: Digireads.com Publishing, 2005), 150, (accessible online at http://books.google.com/books?id=p-BdIAFBYPgC&pg=PA150&lpg=PA150&dq#v=onepage&q&f=false).

II. Answers About God, the Creator

1. Steven Weinberg, *Facing Up* (Cambridge, MA: Harvard University Press, 2012), 242.
2. Candace Adams, "Leading Nanoscientist Builds Big Faith," *Baptist Standard*, March 15, 2002.
3. These five points are summarized from my interview with William Lane Craig in Lee Strobel, *The Case for Faith* (Grand Rapids, MI: 2000), 75–84.
4. Stephen Hawking and Roger Penrose, *The Nature of Space and Time* (Princeton, NJ: Princeton University Press, 2010), 20.

5. Lee Strobel, *The Case for Faith,* 75–76.

6. William Lane Craig, quoted in Lee Strobel, *The Case for a Creator* (Grand Rapids, MI: 2004), 108.

7. Robert Jastrow, *Until the Sun Dies* (New York: W.W. Norton and Company, 1977), 25.

8. Mark Mittelberg, *Confident Faith: Building a Firm Foundation for Your Beliefs* (Carole Stream, IL: Tyndale House, 2013), 177–78.

9. Robin Collins, from our interview in *The Case for a Creator,* 133.

10. Ibid., 134.

11. For a fuller discussion with Robin Collins, including other examples of fine-tuning, see chapter 6 of *The Case for a Creator,* 125.

12. My full interview with Michael Behe is presented in chapter 6 of *The Case for a Creator,* 193.

13. Michael Denton, *Evolution: A Theory in Crisis* (Chevy Chase, MD: Adler & Adler, 1986), 334.

14. Ibid., 318.

15. Quoted in Larry Witham, *By Design,* 172.

16. Strobel, *The Case for a Creator,* 244.

17. Mark Mittelberg, *The Questions Christians Hope No One Will Ask (With Answers)* (Tyndale: Carol Stream, IL: 2010), summarized from chapter 2.

18. Strobel, *The Case for Faith,* 94.

III. *Answers About the Bible*

1. Lee Strobel, *The Case for Christ* (Grand Rapids, MI: Zondervan, 1998), 33.

2. A. N. Sherwin-White, *Roman Society and Roman Law in the New Testament* (Oxford: Clarendon Press, 1963), 188–91.

3. Strobel, *The Case for Christ*, 33–34.

4. Dan Brown, *The Da Vinci Code* (Second Anchor Books Mass-Market Edition 2009; Random House, New York, original copyright 2003), 305.

5. Tryggve N. D. Mettinger, *The Riddle of Resurrection* (Stockholm: Almqvist & Wicksell, 2001), 221.

6. Strobel, *The Case for Christ*, 66.

7. F. F. Bruce, *The New Testament Documents: Are They Reliable?* (Eerdmans, Grand Rapids, MI: 1978), 21.

8. Strobel, *The Case for Christ*, 67.

9. N. T. Wright, *Judas and the Gospel of Jesus* (Grand Rapids, MI: Baker, 2006), 33–34.

10. Robert J. Miller, ed., *The Complete Gospels: Annotated Scholars Version* (Polebridge Press: Santa Rosa, CA, 1992, 1994), 308.

11. Ibid., 326.

12. Ibid., 322.

13. Strobel, *The Case for Christ*, 177.

14. Strobel, *The Case for Christ*, 179–80.

15. Lee Strobel, *The Case for the Real Jesus* (Grand Rapids, MI: Zondervan, 2007), 197–98.

16. Gary Habermas, *The Historical Jesus* (Nashville: Thomas Nelson, 1988).

17. Strobel, *The Case for Christ*, 91.

18. Ibid., 86–87.

19. Ibid., 87.

20. Clifford A. Wilson, *Rocks, Relics and Biblical Reliability* (Grand Rapids, MI: Zondervan, 1977), 42.

21. William F. Albright, *Archaeology and the Religion of Israel* (Baltimore, MD: Johns Hopkins Press, 1953), 176. This interview with Norman Geisler is in Strobel, *The Case for Faith*, 128–29.

22. Colin J. Hemer, *The book of Acts in the Setting of Hellenistic History* (Winona Lake, IN: Eisenbrauns, 1990).

23. William M. Ramsay, *St. Paul the Traveler and the Roman Citizen* (Grand Rapids, MI: Baker, 1982), 8.

24. A. N. Sherwin-White, *Roman Society and Roman Law in the New Testament* (Oxford: Clarendon Press, 1963), 189. This interview with Norman Geisler is in Strobel, *The Case for Faith*, 129–30.

25. Strobel, *The Case for a Creator*, 86.

26. My full interview with Daniel Wallace can be read in "Challenge #2" in Strobel, *The Case for the Real Jesus*, 65.

27. Bart D. Ehrman, *Misquoting Jesus* (San Francisco: HarperSanFrancisco, 2005), 7.

28. Ibid., 89–90.

29. See discussion with Daniel Wallace in "Challenge #2" in Strobel *The Case for the Real Jesus*, especially 85–87.

30. Strobel, *The Case for the Real Jesus*, 81.

IV. Answers About Jesus

1. Matthew 1:22–23 and Luke 1:3.

2. Lee Strobel, *The Case for the Real Jesus* (Grand Rapids, MI: Zondervan, 2007), 179.

3. Thomas Boslooper, *The Virgin Birth* (Philadelphia: Westminster, 1962), 135, quoted in Robert Gromacki, *The Virgin Birth* (Grand Rapids, MI: Kregel, 1974, 2002), 211.

4. Joseph Knabenbauer, *Evang. S. Matt.*, I, 104, quoted in by Charles G., Herbermann, *The Catholic Encyclopedia* (Charleston, SC: Nabu Press, 2010), 419.

5. Lee Strobel, *The Case for Christ* (Grand Rapids, MI: Zondervan, 1998), 140–41.

6. William Lane Craig, *The Son Rises* (Chicago: Moody Press, 1981), 140.

7. My interview with Dr. Gary Collins is in Strobel, *The Case for Christ*, 144.

8. Strobel, *The Case for the Real Jesus,* 255.

9. My full interview with Dr. Alexander Metherell is in chapter 11 of Strobel, *The Case for Christ*, 191.

10. J. E. Holoubek, and A. E. Holoubek, "Blood, Sweat and Fear: 'A Classification of Hematidrosis,'" *Journal of Medicine* 1996, 27 (3–4): 115–33, http://www.ncbi.nlm.nih.gov/pubmed/8982961.

11. Gerd Lüdemann, *The Resurrection of Christ: A Historical Inquiry* (Amherst, NY: Prometheus Books, 2004), 50.

12. Strobel, *The Case for Christ*, 90–91.

13. Gary Habermas, *The Historical Jesus* (Nashville: Thomas Nelson, 1988).

14. Strobel, *The Case for Christ*, 239.

15. Ibid., 238–39.

16. F. F. Bruce, *The New Testament Documents: Are They Reliable?* (Eerdmans, Grand Rapids, MI: 1978), 12.

17. Strobel, *The Case for the Real Jesus*, 115.
18. James D. G. Dunn, *Jesus Remembered* (Grand Rapids, MI: Eerdmans, 2003), 855.
19. Strobel, *The Case for Christ*, 241–42.

V. Answers to Other Challenges to Christianity

1. D. T. Niles, quoted in Paul Little, *Know Why You Believe* (Downers Grove, IL: InterVarsity Press, 1988), 145.
2. Strobel, *The Case for Faith* (Grand Rapids, MI: 2000), 51–52.
3. Mark Mittelberg, *The Questions Christians Hope No One Will Ask (With Answers)*, (Carol Stream, IL: Tyndale, 2010), 18.
4. Strobel, *The Case for Faith*, 80.
5. Mark Mittelberg, *The Questions Christians Hope No One Will Ask (With Answers)*, 20.
6. These quotes of J. P. Moreland are drawn from my interview with him in Strobel, *The Case for Faith*, 173, 175, 192.
7. Ronald H. Nash, *Is Jesus the Only Savior?* (Grand Rapids, MI: Zondervan, 1994), 165.
8. For an example of this basic defense, see Norman Geisler, *Baker Encyclopedia of Christian Apologetics* (Grand Rapids, MI: Baker Books, 1999), 730–31.
9. Ibid., 732.
10. This is a response I've heard Mark Mittelberg give frequently in Q & A sessions we teach together.

VI. Postlude: Turning Answers into Action

1. Michael Shermer, *How We Believe* (New York: W.H. Freeman, 2000), 123.
2. C. S. Lewis, *God in the Dock* (Copyright 1970, By the Trustees of the Estate of C. S. Lewis; Grand Rapids, MI: Eerdmans, reprinted in 2001), 101.

Recommended Resources

Lee Strobel, *The Case for Christ*, (Grand Rapids, MI: Zondervan, 1998).

Lee Strobel, *The Case for Faith*, (Grand Rapids, MI: Zondervan, 2000).

Lee Strobel, *The Case for a Creator*, (Grand Rapids, MI: Zondervan, 2004).

Lee Strobel, *The Case for the Real Jesus*, (Grand Rapids, MI: Zondervan, 2007).

Note: Student and Kids editions of these *Case* books also available

Lee Strobel, *The Case for Grace*, (Grand Rapids, MI: Zondervan, 2014).

Lee Strobel, *The Case for Christ Study Bible*, (Grand Rapids, MI: Zondervan, 2010).

Mark Mittelberg, *Confident Faith: Building a Firm Foundation for Your Beliefs*, (Carol Stream, IL: Tyndale, 2013).

Mark Mittelberg, *The Questions Christians Hope No One Will Ask (With Answers)*, (Carol Stream, IL: Tyndale, 2010).

Mark Mittelberg, *The Reason Why: Faith Makes Sense,* (Carol Stream, IL: Tyndale, 2011).

William Lane Craig, *On Guard: Defending Your Faith with Reason and Precision,* (Colorado Springs, CO: David C. Cook, 2010).

William Lane Craig, *Reasonable Faith,* (Wheaton, IL: Crossway, 2008).

Josh and Sean McDowell *More Than a Carpenter,* (Carol Stream, IL: Tyndale, 2009).

J. Warner Wallace, *Cold-Case Christianity,* (Colorado Springs, CO: David C. Cook, 2013).

Gary R. Habermas and Michael R. Licona, *The Case for the Resurrection of Jesus,* (Grand Rapids, MI: Kregel, 2004).

Norman L. Geisler and Frank Turek, *I Don't Have Enough Faith to Be an Atheist,* (Wheaton, IL: Crossway, 2004).

C. S. Lewis, *Mere Christianity,* (New York City, NY: Macmillan, 1952).

Meet Lee Strobel

Atheist-turned-Christian Lee Strobel, the former award-winning legal editor of the *Chicago Tribune*, is a *New York Times* best-selling author of more than twenty books and serves as Professor of Christian Thought at Houston Baptist University.

Described in the *Washington Post* as "one of the evangelical community's most popular apologists," Lee shared the Christian Book of the Year award in 2005 for a curriculum he coauthored with Garry Poole. Lee also won Gold Medallions for *The Case for Christ*, *The Case for Faith*, and *The Case for a Creator*. His latest works include his first novel, *The Ambition*, and *The Case for Christ Study Bible*. His website is www.LeeStrobel.com.

Lee graduated from the University of Missouri (bachelor of Journalism) and Yale Law School (master of Studies in Law). As a journalist at the *Chicago Tribune* and other newspapers, he won Illinois' highest honor for public service journalism from United Press International. He also led a team that received UPI's top award for investigative reporting in Illinois.

After studying the evidence for Jesus, Lee became a Christian in 1981. He later served as a teaching pastor at two of America's largest churches, leaving to host the national network TV program *Faith Under Fire*.

Along with Mark Mittelberg and Bill Hybels, Lee also coauthored the *Becoming a Contagious Christian* course, which has trained a million and a half Christians on how to naturally and effectively talk with others about Jesus.

Lee and Leslie have been married for forty-one years and live in Colorado. Their daughter, Alison, is a novelist and teaches English at a Christian school. With a doctorate in theology, their son, Kyle, has authored several books and is a professor at Grand Canyon University in Phoenix, Arizona.